GEORGE WALLACE
IN WISCONSIN

GEORGE WALLACE
IN **WISCONSIN**

THE DIVISIVE CAMPAIGNS THAT SHAPED
A CIVIL RIGHTS LEGACY

BEN HUBING

THE
History
PRESS

Published by The History Press
Charleston, SC
www.historypress.com

Front cover: Wallace supporters with pennant and African American protestors: © Milwaukee Journal Sentinel, USA TODAY NETWORK. *inset*: George Wallace. *Photo by Archie Lieberman, used with permission. Back cover*: Commandos surrounding Wallace campaign materials. *Wisconsin Historical Society, WHI-(X3)37639.*

First published 2022

Manufactured in the United States

ISBN 9781467151375

Library of Congress Control Number: 2021950578

To my wife, Nickie; my parents; and my three boys. Thank you for all the support and sacrifice that made this book possible.

Of those men who have overturned the liberties of republics, the greatest number have begun their career by paying an obsequious court to the people, commencing demagogues and ending tyrants.
—Alexander Hamilton

It is certain, in any case, that ignorance, allied with power, is the most ferocious enemy justice can have.
—James Baldwin

CONTENTS

ACKNOWLEDGEMENTS

I n the midst of a historic pandemic at a time when our nation seems more divided than ever, it has been interesting to retrace George Wallace's campaign stops across the Badger State. In some ways, it is reassuring to see that the times we are in are not unprecedented. Yet Wallace's candidacy and the divisions it fostered in Wisconsin have cautionary parallels to the perilous moment we find ourselves in today.

I would like to express gratitude to many who have made this book possible. I am incredibly grateful to Dr. Lewis Larsen and the staff at the James Madison Memorial Foundation, who allowed me the opportunity to complete my graduate studies, where I landed on the topic of this book.

Thanks to the faculty and staff at the University of Wisconsin–Milwaukee for maintaining a rigorous and supportive learning environment in the midst of a global pandemic. I am especially grateful to Dr. Joe Austin, whose graduate seminar first introduced me to Wallace's speech in a packed Serb Hall on Milwaukee's south side. It was his course that got me thinking about how such a campaign was possible in Wisconsin and what it might tell us about today. Many thanks to my graduate advisor, Dr. Lex Renda, for his thorough feedback and in helping me fine-tune my manuscript, and Dr. Christine Evans, whose support was integral in completing what would become this book.

It was incredibly challenging gaining access to archives during the pandemic, and I am appreciative of Hermoine Bell-Henderson and Melissa Shriver at the Milwaukee Public Library for their help in accessing microfilm of Black newspapers in Milwaukee that were essential to the project. Thanks also to the Wisconsin State Historical Society for its responsiveness and willingness to provide resources during these difficult times.

I want to express much gratitude to John Rodrigue and the staff at The History Press. As I was a newbie to much of this process, John patiently guided me through publication, answering my many questions. His advice, responsiveness and editorial diligence have been tremendously helpful in creating this book.

Most importantly, I would like to thank my family, whose love and support made this book possible. My parents, Jeff and Lori, have been a constant in my life. I cannot think of a time that they weren't willing to drop what they were doing and support me in a moment's notice. Their love of travel and our family trips opened my eyes to the history all around us, and I will be forever grateful for their unconditional support. My wife, Nickie, is the love of my life and has been a source of unwavering love and support. The work that culminated in this book was a tremendous stress on our family, and I am forever grateful for her carrying that burden. Finally, to my boys, Sammy, Ollie and Timmy. Being their dad is the honor of my life, and it is my hope that the future they find rises above the troubled times of past and present.

STAGE SETTING FOR A SHOWDOWN IN MONTGOMERY AND MILWAUKEE

FEDERALISM AND EQUAL PROTECTION DIVERGE IN WISCONSIN

In 1854, national forces had engulfed local events in Wisconsin. An enslaved man named Joshua Glover had escaped from Missouri and settled in Racine to live a quiet but free life two years earlier. However, when Glover's former enslaver discovered his whereabouts, he obtained an affidavit and, with the help of a posse, violently captured Glover and brought him to a Milwaukee jail to hold him before they were to return to Missouri.[1]

The federal Fugitive Slave Act of 1850 required that escaped enslaved people be returned to enslavers in the South and criminalized the act of aiding an enslaved person find freedom. However, Wisconsin had a strong network of abolitionists who opposed slavery and actively helped assist escaped enslaved people via the Underground Railroad. Glover's detention mobilized these abolitionists, and after a meeting outside the jail led by abolitionist journalist Sherman Booth, the crowd kicked down the outer door, used a beam as a battering ram and freed Glover from the prison cell in a dramatic act of defiance against the federal statute.[2]

Glover escaped to Canada, but his freedom built momentum in Wisconsin, culminating with the state supreme court ruling that federal courts could not imprison Booth, declaring the Fugitive Slave Act unconstitutional and in essence nullifying federal law.[3] This shocking rebuke of federal authority led to a series of clashes between the federal and state courts, concluding with the U.S. Supreme Court, led by Chief Justice Roger Taney, reversing the Wisconsin Supreme Court's decision, arguing that the state courts were lower in the hierarchy and that federal laws overruled the states.[4]

On the eve of the Civil War, in the midst of a federal crisis on civil rights, Wisconsin abolitionists and the state supreme court utilized federalism to advocate for the equal protection of the state's Black residents. Activists were willing to defy federal statutes and authority to ensure equal rights for African Americans. A century later, national momentum around civil rights would reemerge in the United States, but this time, federalism and equal protection would be ideals at odds. Black leaders and activists would begin to demand greater federal authority to ensure the rights of African Americans in the Badger State, while proponents of federalism would find an outsider to amplify their desires to thwart federal authority and preserve the unequal status quo.

"SEGREGATION FOREVER!"

When the newly elected governor of Alabama stepped up to the podium on January 14, 1963, George Wallace began his career with the defiant pledge to protect "Segregation now! Segregation tomorrow! Segregation forever!"[5] After facing defeat four years earlier in his gubernatorial race, Wallace came away with the lesson that he had been "out-n——ed" by his opponent and vowed to take an aggressive stance on racial issues. His campaign and early years as governor were defined by his opposition to Black equality and any federal role in protecting the rights of African Americans in his state. From the beginning, Wallace intended to tap into feelings of grievance and powerlessness among white Alabamians following the Supreme Court's 1954 decision *Brown v. Board of Education of Topeka*, which declared segregation in the public schools was unconstitutional.[6] Wallace vehemently denied being a racist but proudly defended being a segregationist. His gripe, he claimed, was not with Black Alabamians, but with a federal government intervening in the laws and customs of his state. According to historian Dan Carter, Wallace replaced the "age old southern cry of 'N——, n——'" with "political equivalents of apple pie and motherhood: the rights of private property, community control, neighborhood schools, and union seniority."[7]

While the prejudices and personal beliefs of the governor may not be knowable with complete certainty, one Wallace biographer aptly stated that whether he was a bigot or dog whistling to win support, "In the end, an opportunist is no better than a racist, and less honest."[8]

STAND IN THE SCHOOLHOUSE DOOR

While a poor boy from a small Alabama town called Clio might have seen his ascendancy to governor of his state as the pinnacle, Wallace had his eyes on the presidency from the beginning. And as it would happen, events in his home state would propel the first-term governor into the national spotlight.

His first major showdown with the federal government came a few months later in the fall of 1962, as the integration of the University of Alabama became an issue for the governor to employ his federalism-based rhetoric. When the Kennedy administration put pressure on Wallace to comply with the federal court order to integrate by sending Attorney General Bobby Kennedy to meet with Wallace, the dialogue and any hopes of cooperation evaporated.[9] Wallace pledged to "stand in the schoolhouse door" to prevent federal troops from integrating the university against the wishes of the state government. Despite his rhetoric, federal judge Seybourn H. Lynn granted the Justice Department an injunction that prevented Wallace from interfering with the admission of two Black students, James Hood and Vivian Malone. The judge pointed out that the U.S. Supreme Court "had rejected the doctrine of interposition" and the governor lacked constitutional grounds to "obstruct or prevent execution of lawful orders of a court of the United States."[10]

On June 11, 1963, Kennedy sent Assistant Attorney General Nick Katzenbach to the campus to ensure the students were allowed to enroll, which led to a public confrontation between Wallace and the Justice Department. Wallace greeted Katzenbach at a podium, ready to make a statement with the media present. Wallace claimed that state sovereignty was violated by "an illegal usurpation of power by the Central Government" and ended with his pledge to "denounce and forbid this illegal and unwarranted action by the Central Government."[11] Invoking the Tenth Amendment, Wallace claimed that states had reserved authority over the operation of schools and that forcible integration of schools was "an attempt to subordinate the rights of self-determination by individuals and states to the wishes of the federal government."[12] Despite the rhetoric, Kennedy federalized the Alabama National Guard, and Wallace had no choice but to back down.[13]

The same night as the showdown in Tuscaloosa, President Kennedy addressed the American people over television, calling for Congress pass a civil rights bill to provide increased federal authority to end de jure segregation and outlaw discrimination based on race, sex, creed or national origin.[14] Wallace blasted the proposal as akin to "military dictatorship" and a violation of federal and executive power.[15] Despite his inability to stop Hood and Malone from enrolling at the University of Alabama, Wallace was determined to defeat the pending Civil Rights Bill.

Wallace continued his conflict with federal officials a few months later in Birmingham, again coming up on the losing end. He had pressured city officials to close their public schools rather than integrate, but as he did in Tuscaloosa, he was forced to back away from his defiant efforts in the face of court orders to change course.[16] But it was the bombing of the Sixteenth Street Baptist Church on September 15 that increased tension between the federal and state officials. Wallace blamed the bombing on "the Supreme Court, the Kennedy administration and civil rights agitators," while Kennedy became emboldened to push for a federal civil rights bill, viewing the state and business leaders as ambivalent in fostering the "climate which Kennedy was convinced had led to the death of four little Black girls."[17]

MILWAUKEE'S INNER CORE

Almost 850 miles north of Montgomery, the civil rights movement was gaining momentum in Milwaukee. Since the 1920s, poverty, white flight and municipal neglect had, according to one study, left the Black neighborhoods of the city of Milwaukee "dying at its core." Milwaukee's Black residents outpaced their white counterparts in infant mortality, welfare use, joblessness and convictions, and they lagged behind in education and homeownership. Milwaukee's Black population remained relatively small until 1950, when it increased from 13,000 five years earlier to nearly 22,000. That number tripled by 1960 to over 62,000 and rose to over 100,000 people by 1970.[18]

While the Black organizations, churches and clubs worked to address the countless challenges of the Black community, they remained "politically powerless, economically impotent, largely ignored and completely marginalized through the 1950s."[19] De facto segregation in Milwaukee was equal to that of Birmingham and other southern cities. Socialist mayor Frank Zeidler empathized with the Black community and promoted policies of slum clearance and public housing to help rescue the "submerged people" of the inner core.[20] This support led to a nasty reelection campaign for the mayor in 1956, in which his opponents tried to stir up opposition with false accusations that he planned to "import African Americans into their neighborhoods" and that he encouraged migration of Black southerners by posting billboards. In what *Time* magazine blasted as "The Shame of

Milwaukee," the campaign slogan of Milton McGuire, Zeidler's opponent, called for "an honest white man for mayor." Although Zeidler won reelection, he would not run again in 1960 and was replaced by Henry Maier, who favored a "go slow" approach with regards to civil rights.[21] The response to Zeidler demonstrated that there was political capital and support among white Milwaukeeans to opposing and thwarting civil rights.

Emergence of the "Selma of the North"

While the most high-profile moments of the civil rights movement were still years away, the movement's emergence ran parallel to George Wallace's ascendance in Alabama. It can be argued that the genesis of the organized movement for greater equality for African Americans was the 1958 murder of Daniel Bell, a twenty-two-year-old Black man who fled after being pulled over by police, likely because he did not want to get caught driving without a license. The police fatally shot Bell in the back at close range, and the officers planted a knife and fabricated a coverup story.[22]

Bell's tragic death was "the signal shot for the black freedom movement in Milwaukee," sparking organized community protests.[23] The Milwaukee NAACP chapter, allied with clergy and community leaders, clashed with more conservative old guard Black leaders about the wisdom in public demonstrations. Eventually, Calvin Sherard established the Crusaders Civic and Social League, which worked to promote Black businesses, increase Black employment and improve police relations. The group began picketing Milwaukee businesses, eventually affiliating with A. Philip Randolph's Negro American Labor Council.[24] While gaining only limited success and community support, the MNALC organized "the first demonstrations in Milwaukee where people hit the streets and went to jail for their freedoms."[25]

As Wallace stood in the schoolhouse door and Kennedy called on the nation to act, a Black paper, the *Milwaukee Star*, called the president's speech "one of the greatest speeches of all time" but made no connection to the emerging civil rights movement in Milwaukee.[26] Civil rights groups picketed outside city hall, calling for federal civil rights legislation, while Mayor Maier called for the "go slow" approach. By 1963, the Congress of Racial Equality (CORE) had founded a Milwaukee chapter, and it now pushed for a nonviolent approach that was nonetheless more aggressive than the cautious approach of old guard Black leaders. The new group's first test was in response to a comment from a sausage company president, Fred Lins, who told a reporter that preventing the "ignorant poor" from migrating to Milwaukee would save taxpayers from spending on welfare. Lins was a member of Mayor Maier's Social Development Commission, tasked with addressing urban problems and gaining federal funds for urban renewal. MCORE began its first campaign with picketing, sit-ins, letter writing and phone-ins. While Lins remained on the commission, the protests unified the Black community, as it became apparent to the more cautious old guard that appeals to white leaders were not fruitful and direct action was needed.

In early 1964, activists began focusing on school integration as their primary issue. Despite the landmark decision *Brown v. Board* ending school segregation a decade earlier, Milwaukee schools remained largely segregated. Led by Lloyd Barbee, activists pushed for "system-wide racial balance" and opposed Milwaukee Public Schools' policy of "intact busing," in which Black students were brought to white schools but kept as a separate unit that was taught separately. The policy even went so far as to return the Black children home for lunch to avoid sharing a cafeteria with white students.[27] As Wallace entered the Wisconsin primary, Barbee and others created a new organization called the Milwaukee United School Integration Committee (MUSIC), meant to unite various civil rights groups under an umbrella organization to tackle school integration.[28]

The crescendo of the civil rights movement in Milwaukee was still four years away in 1963. But the stage was set for the showdown between Wallace and the state's Black leaders. Groups formed in reaction to local injustices and inequities, but the Alabamian would be a formidable national opponent. Both sides would employ different constitutional justifications to achieve their goals.

2

1964 WISCONSIN DEMOCRATIC PRIMARY

Wallace Weaponizes Federalism

After increased national notoriety following his showdown with Kennedy and the federal government, Wallace launched the first of four presidential campaigns in 1964, challenging incumbent Lyndon Johnson for the Democratic nomination. Wallace entered three primary contests, starting first in Wisconsin. Perceived as a progressive bastion, the Badger State seemed an unlikely staging ground for a racist segregationist to rally support. However, when the contest concluded, Wallace had won nearly 30 percent of the primary vote, shocking the nation and putting the passage of the Civil Rights Bill in doubt.

While there is a broad consensus on the historical context leading up to Wallace's unlikely victory in the 1964 Democratic primary, there is disagreement about the factors that led to his success in the Badger State. James Gregory points to the importance of migrations of Black and white southerners in creating a climate of racial resentment similar to Wallace's Alabama.[29] Dan Carter focuses on the importance of white rage and backlash to Johnson's policies, notably the pending Civil Rights Act.[30] Jody Carlson argues that Wallace tapped into a larger feeling of powerlessness voters felt regarding the federal government.[31] Richard Haney focuses more on the negative reaction Wallace received than other historians and tempers the notion and implications of a broad victory for Wallace in the Wisconsin primary.[32] Margaret Conway utilizes demographic data to discern where Wallace received the broadest support, and Stephen

Leahy attempts to debunk the notion that working-class Poles with racial prejudices were a significant source of Wallace support.[33] While all of these sources attempt to discern whom Wallace won over in the Wisconsin Primary, they do not address how Wallace was able win over such a large base of white Wisconsinites.

How was such a run possible? Wallace employed powerful rhetoric that utilized federalism in opposition to the national bill. His candidacy skirted around overt racism, focusing on a vague concept of states' rights, which many saw as disingenuous dog whistling. Wallace's campaign turned the Wisconsin primary into a referendum on the Civil Rights Bill, with a response much more mixed than many national politicians and pundits expected. While many newspapers, state leaders and Wisconsinites strongly opposed Wallace's campaign, there is ample evidence showing support for his rhetoric and argument of federalism. These differing perceptions and perspectives in the midst of the monthlong primary campaign foreshadowed the emergence of tension by the late 1960s and early 1970s, when open housing and school integration propelled Milwaukee and Wisconsin into the larger national debate on the extent to which states could and should comply to federal requirements on civil rights.

DISCOURSES OF DISSENT

Immediately following Wallace's attempts at blocking integration at the University of Alabama, he decided to tap into his newfound national profile by bringing his segregationist and states' rights message to campuses north of the Mason-Dixon line. This included stops at several Ivy League colleges on the East Coast, as well as campuses on the West Coast and in the Midwest. During these visits, Wallace downplayed the racism and focused on constitutional critiques.[34] It was this tour that first brought Wallace to the Badger State on February 19, as part of the University of Wisconsin's "distinguished series of lectures—Discourses of Dissent."[35]

His arrival in Milwaukee the day before brought only a handful of supporters and over fifty CORE pickets. Referred to by the *Milwaukee Sentinel* as a "small, fast-talking man," he stated he "believed local government" was "perfectly able to take care of its own affairs."[36] Wallace claimed Wisconsinites would be directly affected by the bill, through centralization of public education, hiring mandates and the loss of union seniority for white workers.[37]

Wallace is picketed at a Milwaukee event during his 1964 campaign. *From the* Capital Times, *reprinted with permission.*

During his lecture in Madison, Wallace railed against the Civil Rights Bill, then being debated in Congress, bringing his states' rights arguments and fear of an overpowering federal government into unfamiliar territory. "[The United States] was never meant to be a unit of one, but a unit of many," Wallace claimed, arguing that the framers who created the Constitution meant for "central government [to be] a servant of the people, and not a master."[38] Wallace, blending states' rights and libertarianism, argued it was this pending Civil Rights Bill that posed a "tyrannical threat to our... governmental structure," and amounted to a "revolution of government against the people."[39] He argued that the law was an assault on private property, which he claimed was an important human right that was being neglected at the expense of civil rights. According to Wallace, social engineers, powerful politicians and the news media were all in league to limit personal freedom.[40] Wallace also claimed that African Americans were better off in Alabama than in Wisconsin, arguing that racial unrest was more peaceful, and provided data he claimed proved wages and education were higher. He claimed to take no issue with fair housing but insisted laws should be passed in Madison, not Washington. Finally, he criticized the Supreme Court for destroying the Constitution and cited Presidents Lincoln, Jackson, Roosevelt and Jefferson as precedents either defying or criticizing the court's actions.[41] At a press conference, Wallace claimed the bill would require a "police state to enforce it."[42] He later told the Madison Rotary Club, "If the people of Wisconsin are not intelligent enough to decide these matters [civil rights]…you might as well abolish state government."[43] Without overtly using racial language, Wallace introduced under the veil of states' rights a fear of an overarching federal bogeyman that in granting equality to African Americans denied white Americans opportunity and liberty.

Wallace's introduction in Wisconsin was mixed. He claimed that Wisconsinites were "well-represented among the letter writers" who were supportive of his beliefs.[44] However, civil rights protesters greeted him on his arrival, holding signs blasting Wallace as "Birmingham's Shame" and declaring "Racists Not Welcome."[45] Over two hundred picketers tried to confront Wallace at the Memorial Union prior to his lecture, with fifteen of them silently protesting from front-row seats during his speech.[46] Wallace did not interact with the protesters; he was whisked out a side door, as would be the case throughout his forthcoming campaign. The next morning, students took red Kool-Aid powder and wrote "F—— Wallace!" on frozen Lake Mendota right outside his hotel room.[47]

The press coverage was generally not positive. A defiant open letter in the *Capital Times* blasted the governor, attacking Wallace for his cruelty to protesters in Alabama compared to his feeble reaction to picketers in Wisconsin and imploring Wallace (who insisted in his speech that Alabamians would defy the Supreme Court's prohibition of prayer in schools) to recall scripture that asked Christians to love their neighbors and do unto others as you would have done unto you.[48] Commentator Miles McMillin argued that Wallace was determined to "thwart the constitutional processes of this country."[49] He also likened Wallace to the antebellum politician Stephen A. Douglas, who used "[states'] rights-property arguments to defend slavery" and compared the fallacy of that argument to Wallace's federalism argument with respect to civil rights.[50]

Despite the protests, negative press and hecklers, the crowd received the speech warmly. Wallace used his humor and quips to disarm his audience (he asked if the pickets would replace singing of "We Shall Overcome" with "Home on the Range") and claimed to be more tolerant than Lincoln because he believed Black people should be able to hold office, vote and serve on juries.[51] According to the *Kenosha News*, the audience was "critical but friendly, with only a scattered 'hiss' or 'boo.'"[52] While another account described the audience as rowdy and heckling, it also noted that many were bewildered by Wallace's unexpected affability, coolness under pressure and ability to downplay overt racism.[53] According to the associate editor of the student newspaper, the *Daily Cardinal*, "He came, he saw, and although there were protests, he conquered." Wallace's press secretary claimed he received a standing ovation at the Madison Rotary Club the next day after predicting an alliance between northern and southern states that would "put this government back on the right track."[54]

The most important supporters that Wallace encountered were Oshkosh natives Lloyd and Delores Herbstreith, who, according to Wallace, "started the ball rolling" in Wisconsin.[55] Both were politically active in conservative politics, supporting a constitutional amendment to eliminate the federal income tax. While they reportedly did not support Wallace's position on civil rights, they believed Wallace's convictions on "states' rights and limited federal government" would resonate in Wisconsin, and they encouraged him to enter the upcoming April 7 presidential primary race.[56] According to Wallace's press secretary, he was already considering such a run, but Wisconsin's relatively easy ballot access and open primary system made such a run conceivable for the first time.[57]

Wallace laid the groundwork for a monthlong campaign in Wisconsin that would "mark the high-water tide against the Civil Rights Bill pending before the U.S. Senate" and propelled the segregationist into the spotlight as a national opponent of civil rights.[58] Wallace learned that his states' rights approach would draw not only media attention and fierce opposition but also support from a receptive audience in Wisconsin.

Stand Up for America: The Campaign Begins

Over the next few weeks, Delores Herbstreith, who would become Wallace's state campaign chair, corralled the requisite number of state delegates, setting the stage for the Alabama governor's dramatic return to Wisconsin on March 6.[59] Flying into Madison, he officially filed papers to enter the Wisconsin primary race.[60] Although President Lyndon Johnson was the presumptive nominee, he had not yet formally declared (nor had any major Republican candidates). This meant in the absence of President Johnson, Wisconsin governor John Reynolds filed as a "favorite son" placeholder. Reynolds was a progressive Democrat who had taken controversial stances on highway construction and in favoring an open housing law. Further muddying the political waters, Wisconsin was an open primary state, meaning that Republicans could cross over and vote for Wallace in the Democratic primary, conceivably to embarrass Reynolds and the Democrats. (No Republicans had yet declared, so GOP placeholder John Byrnes ran unopposed.)[61]

Wallace hoped that the wildcards and unknowns in this race would make it possible for him to garner support from conservative opponents to civil rights, members of the John Birch Society and those dissatisfied with Reynolds and Republicans looking to play spoiler. He challenged Reynolds to a television debate on civil rights (which Reynolds declined).[62] Wallace defiantly claimed a vote for him would be a "protest vote" against federal policies and could help temper the Democratic platform.[63] However, he insisted that segregation would not be a topic of discussion during his candidacy, since each state should decide such issues for itself.[64]

As Wallace departed, promising to return in about a week to begin his campaign, he left the state in shock and disarray. There was immediate concern, both private and public, from Democratic Party officials and politicians, including Wisconsin senator William Proxmire, who feared that Wallace could win considerable support in the primary.[65] State party chairman Louis Hanson denounced Wallace as a "demagogue, state righter, hatemonger, and a member of the 'lunatic fringe.'"[66] There was a call by Hanson for the party (which had personal and ideological divisions in the state) to unify to thwart embarrassment.[67]

The state AFL-CIO denounced Wallace as an anti-labor "carpetbagger."[68] The steering committee of the Greater Milwaukee Conference on Religion and Race pledged to "exert moral force" to defeat the racist governor.[69] CORE chapters, which greeted Wallace with placards condemning him for having "blood on his hands" (a reference to the bombing of the Sixteenth Street Baptist Church that killed four young girls), began planning their next moves.[70] One CORE official referred to Wallace as a "tyrant and a bigot" who "defied the law and government of the nation."[71]

The media backlash to Wallace's campaign was swift and strong. An editor's memo in the *Capital Times* caustically challenged the Alabamian to justify how he could deny taxpaying African Americans in his state equal access to public facilities.[72] An editorial from the *Milwaukee Journal* likened Wallace's campaign to an "invasion," juxtaposing Wisconsin's historic commitment to opposing slavery and racism to the governor's desire to "deny many citizens the full rights granted them by the Constitution."[73] The *Racine Journal Times* declared Wallace unwelcome, claiming his preservation of the "southern way of life" was a mere cover for his "ideology of white supremacy and racial segregation."[74] The *Green Bay Press-Gazette* slammed his candidacy as a foolish stunt that was already "settled by the Civil War."[75] The *Wisconsin State Journal* dismissed Wallace's states' rights claims, arguing that Wisconsin's support of human rights would win in the election.[76] The UW newspaper, the *Daily Cardinal*, endorsed Reynolds, arguing that defeating Wallace would demonstrate to racists that "their day is done."[77] The *Milwaukee Journal* challenged Wallace's states' rights views, asking: "States rights to do what? To disobey the law and federal authority as he has done in Alabama?"[78] The *Kenosha Times* implored readers to resist Wallace's "mischief" by measuring his "ideas, in terms of freedom, opportunity and the traditions and principles…[on which] the government has been built."[79]

There were some signs of interest and possibly support for Wallace, however. In a letter to the editor of the *Eau Claire Daily Telegram*, Leslie Simons compared attacks on Wallace to the crucifixion and implored Republicans to support his candidacy.[80] "An American First, A Republican Second" wrote to the *Green Bay Press-Gazette*, praising Wallace as the "true spirit of our founders who fought for and upheld the Constitution no matter the cost to themselves."[81] While Peter Link conceded that much of what Wallace stands for is "distasteful," Reynolds and his agenda were worse."[82]

The *Eau Claire Daily Telegram* dubbed the primary a "rights referendum."[83] Governor Reynolds canceled a trade mission trip to Europe to actively campaign against Wallace, declaring civil rights a "moral issue of the highest order" and calling on all Wisconsinites to put partisan differences aside to ensure the defeat of the segregationist governor.[84] Before a single rally had been scheduled, it was clear that Wallace's entry into the Wisconsin primary transformed the election from a lethargic afterthought to an electric event with national implications.

LAUNCH IN THE FOX VALLEY

On March 17, Wallace returned to Wisconsin to officially launch his campaign. His sights were set on a heavily Republican region, the Fox River Valley. Wallace opened his campaign in Appleton, the hometown of infamous anti-communist Senator Joseph McCarthy. It was also an area where support for civil rights was shaky, as it was represented by the only Wisconsin congressman to oppose the bill in the House.[85] The strategy was clear: attract conservatives with his states' rights rhetoric and undermine the pending Civil Rights Act.

Wallace supporters greet Wallace upon his arrival in Milwaukee. *From the* Capital Times, *reprinted with permission.*

Upon his arrival (on a plane with a Confederate flag on the side), Wallace reiterated his platform was not that of segregation but "whether the federal government should run the states" and warned that the pending bill (which he branded the "involuntary servitude act") had the potential to give the federal government the authority to "take over practically every phase of local government."[86] He quipped, "[There is] no need to transfer the authority of the Appleton Common Council or the state of Wisconsin to Washington D.C."[87] Wallace challenged listeners to find anything in his record that demonstrated racism or bigotry.[88] He again reiterated how the bill imperiled property rights, particularly the portion that prohibited discrimination in public accommodations.[89] He altered his gubernatorial slogan from "Stand up for Alabama" to "Stand up for America," imploring his audience to take control of their systems, traditions and ideals.[90]

His arrival at Oshkosh State College (now known as UW–Oshkosh) was far more adversarial, as he confronted student picketers, many carrying signs and some darkening their faces in solidarity with African Americans. Wallace continued to rail against the Civil Rights Bill, arguing it would make the president a dictator of a police state, abolish jury trials, destroy freedom of labor and limit local control of schools.[91] According to the *Capital Times*, there were forty negative and only five supportive signs packed into the rowdy student union. Protesters heckled and chanted at the governor, blocking his car until police cleared his path to exit.[92] Wallace then met with fifteen members of the Oshkosh Ministerial Association, which asked pointed questions and bluntly challenged Wallace's views.[93] In this exchange, Wallace claimed that racists and segregationists were not the same thing because a racist "dislikes another man because he is black—he despises the handiwork of God. A segregationist is a man who knows [that God] separated us Himself at the beginning."[94] Wallace charged that "property rights are human rights too, and the Civil Rights Bill threatened the destruction of property rights."[95] He went on to call northern leaders hypocrites for denying the continued existence of segregation in cities like Milwaukee.[96]

Before Wallace even arrived in Appleton, two supporters of the governor from Milwaukee claimed to have received upward of four dozen threatening phone calls and were harassed by picketers from the Black community outside their homes.[97] The Wallace supporters claimed that while they were

Wallace is confronted by hecklers and protesters at his campaign stop at Oshkosh State College. *From the* Capital Times. *Reprinted with permission.*

opposed to segregation, "the rights of mankind to go and come and do what he wants without interfering with the rights of others" were violated by this invasion of privacy.[98]

Governor Reynolds also hit the campaign trail, trying to rally support for his stand-in candidacy for President Johnson. He warned that support for Wallace would embolden racists and hatemongers and put the Civil Rights Bill in peril. There was fear among Democrats that a strong showing for Wallace would make Wisconsin the "laughingstock of the nation."[99] The governor's commission on human rights issued a statement calling on voters to reject Wallace's "brand of racism," which was "not acceptable in Wisconsin."[100] Labor unions responded to his Fox Valley visit by sending out fourteen thousand letters to union members outlining his "sorry record with labor groups."[101]

Local papers again came out with almost united criticism of Wallace's opening salvos. The *Sheboygan Press* criticized Alabama's low rankings in education and said he should be "repudiated and sent back to Alabama."[102] The *Eau Claire Daily Telegram* blasted Wallace's state for being the beneficiary of more federal funds than Wisconsin, supplementing the southern state's paltry state taxes.[103] The traditionally apolitical *Catholic Herald Citizen* featured an editorial from Father John T. O'Connor condemning the governor as a "moral evil" known for promoting "racism which has been specifically condemned by Pope Pius XI."[104] The *Marshfield News-Herald* referred to Wallace's candidacy as a joke, beseeching him to return to Alabama, but also worried that local residents appeared willing to vote for Wallace to embarrass Reynolds.[105] The *Capital Times* referred to the campaign as "inept," wandering around without "knowing the language."[106] The *Racine Journal-Times* argued that Wallace's idea of conservatism was a "one party police state" and states' rights meant that whites in a state were allowed to reduce the "negro population to second class citizens."[107] The *Appleton Post-Crescent* pointed out that despite Wallace's condemnation of the Civil Rights Bill, the reason such a law was necessary is that states like Alabama failed to protect Black citizens. The piece pointed to literacy tests, glacial changes in school integration and the killing of four innocent girls in Birmingham as evidence of Alabama's intransigence.[108] An article in the *Green Bay Press-Gazette* criticized Wallace for being cautious and unaggressive in his rhetoric in opposition to segregation and "acting like an intruder" in the northern state.[109]

When Wallace arrived in Milwaukee en route to Appleton, there were no pickets, but around twenty-nine supporters carried signs that said "Wallace for Prez" and "Welcome to Wisconsin."[110] According to the *Appleton Post-Crescent*, Wallace's speech to the rotary club, which ended in a standing ovation, "shattered" attendance records.[111] Wallace claimed in his speeches that he received overwhelmingly positive mail from Wisconsinites in the early days of his candidacy. His press secretary quantified the number, stating that 95 percent of his mail and calls were favorable.[112] It was this surge in support, Wallace believed, that shifted his initial mindset of simply running as a protest vote now seriously seeking the presidency to ensure Wisconsinites had the "right to make and enforce [their] own laws."[113]

Supporters of the governor at Oshkosh State College touted signs calling for "Rights for Whites" and demanding an end to the "Washington Power Grab."[114] Proponents also wrote into local papers, including Philip Paulson, who blasted Reynolds for not debating Wallace and for his belief that "moral issues can be solved with harsh federal legislation rather than successful, moderate community efforts."[115] Verne Kaub wrote to the *Wisconsin State Journal*, maintaining the importance of states' rights and the Constitution and calling on Reynolds to identify scriptural support for the integration or "mongrelization" of the races.[116] The *Marshfield News-Herald* argued that liberals were hypocritical in trying to shame and silence Wallace. It asked rhetorically, "What is wrong with letting Mr. Wallace say his piece, and leaving the character judgments to the voters?"[117]

As Wallace's campaign began to take shape, the fault lines in the Badger State were being laid bare. Wallace found support and a receptive audience in the Fox River Valley for his states' rights rhetoric, but forces began to take shape to call out the hypocrisy and disingenuousness of his candidacy. Establishment Democrats, liberals, civil rights groups, labor unions and religious groups were wading into the political waters to challenge Wallace.

Emerging Momentum

Wallace returned to Wisconsin on March 23, traveling to Whitewater State College (now UW–Whitewater) and by St. Norbert's College in Green Bay on the following day. Wallace renewed his challenge to Governor Reynolds to debate the merits of the Civil Rights Bill in front of a packed auditorium in Whitewater.[118] Over 1,300 mostly enthusiastic students listened as Wallace argued that his supporters were accused of being "haters" because of their belief in fiscal responsibility, the rights of states and "the basic precepts of the Founding Fathers."[119] He promised to "preserve constitutional government and state's sovereignty" and pledged that differences between states and their residents necessitated freedom in making local decisions without excessive federal interference.[120] In Green Bay, he reiterated concerns of an overreaching federal government, warning the bill would supersede existing Wisconsin laws, lead to forced busing of students and loss of local control of schools and deny Wisconsin businesses the right to "take anybody except those with green hair."[121]

While in Green Bay, Wallace vainly tried to shore up a bipartisan constituency that dominated the state: Packers fans. Green Bay quarterback Bart Starr was a native Alabamian and an alumnus of the University of Alabama. Wallace's campaign manager, Bill Jones, reached out to Starr to set up a meeting with the governor, but when it fell through, the campaign leaked a telegram to the press. In the note, Starr apologized for not being able to meet, saying he hoped to see Wallace another time and offering his service. Starr was furious when he found out about the telegram and made it clear that the campaign released the correspondence without his consent. Starr stated flatly that he and his wife, Cherry, had no plans to endorse or campaign with Wallace, claiming to want "nothing to do with them."[122]

After taking a short trip to D.C. to debate the governor of Maryland (whom Wallace would face in a primary weeks later), Wallace returned to Wisconsin on March 27 and spoke in Eau Claire and Chippewa Falls, hoping to garner conservative support in the northwestern part of the state. Speaking to a crowd of eight hundred in a junior high school auditorium, Wallace continued his assault on the Civil Rights Bill (which he retorted was 10 percent civil rights and 90 percent a federal power grab), arguing that segregation was a matter for the states, downplaying race and claiming "local officials [should] enforce Wisconsin laws, not Washington."[123] He speculated that nondiscrimination laws would deny homeowners the right to sell their homes to whomever they pleased and in order to ensure fair hiring practices, "some people" (ostensibly white workers) would have to lose their jobs.[124] Wallace worried that the attorney general would assume dictatorial powers over the states, and he claimed to be "sick of those people in Washington trying to control every part of a person's life."[125] Trying to muster support, Wallace stated at a press conference that "an integrationist could vote for him" because his campaign was centered on states' rights.[126]

As Wallace's campaign gained momentum, it found increasing numbers of picketers and protesters, many wielding signs with messages such as "Segregation is Wrong" and "There is no room for hate here."[127] NAACP members held a rally in Milwaukee, marching with pickets and singing "We

Wallace encounters some colorful signs that protest his stop at St. Norbert's College in De Pere. *AP photo.*

Shall Overcome."[128] At St. Norbert College, students organized a silent treatment for the Alabama governor, distributing pamphlets that reminded audience members that "silence is golden" and imploring students on the Catholic campus not to sink to the segregationist's level by becoming disorderly. This marked one of the few times on the campaign that Wallace lost his "platform composure"; protestors flustered the Alabamian with the collective cold shoulder.[129] A Black student in the audience challenged Wallace, demanding to know "if he considered Negroes human beings."[130] On March 27, an advertisement was taken out in the *Eau Claire Daily Telegram*, signed by dozens of clergy of all faiths, denouncing Wallace's "system of racial hatred and…segregation" as "morally evil."[131] Alabama writer and journalist William Bradford Huie, a Wallace critic, came up to Wisconsin and spoke publicly wherever possible to dissuade voters from selecting his state's governor.[132]

Reynolds, claiming Wallace was the candidate of "racists and bigots," warned that it would be a "black day for the state of Wisconsin" if voters did not get out the vote.[133] Senator Gaylord Nelson weighed in for the first time in the campaign, blasting Wallace as damaging "the doctrine of states rights" by creating a police state in Alabama.[134] Nelson argued that not only did the Civil Rights Bill not take away rights (as Wallace claimed), but also it was needed to "restore rights taken away by Wallace's troopers in Alabama."[135] Wisconsin senator William Proxmire branded Wallace's candidacy "a racist move to kill the civil rights bill," while praising four conservative Republican congressmen from Wisconsin who voted in favor of the bill.[136]

The *La Crosse Tribune* editorial board worried that Wallace was using the Wisconsin primary for his own perverse goals and that it was the Badger State that would be the loser.[137] Carol Kiley of Menasha wrote to the *Appleton Post-Crescent*, blasting Wallace's racism and blaming him for the bombing deaths in Birmingham.[138] "An Old Timer" warned readers of the *Eau Claire Leader-Telegram* that a Wallace win in Wisconsin might lead to a poll tax in the state.[139]

The *Sheboygan Press* doubted that voters would be mesmerized by his antics.[140] The *Milwaukee Journal* implored leaders in both parties (including Republicans who were founded in the Badger State pledging to "the full use of power, resources, and leadership of the federal level eliminate discrimination based on race") to reaffirm Wisconsin's "record of dedication to freedom and equal rights" by actively speaking out against Wallace.[141] Several papers, including the *Capital Times* and *Milwaukee Journal* and *Sentinel*, "fact checked" Wallace by publishing exposés on what was actually in the bill and what was not.[142]

Despite the negative press and protests, Wallace continued to find supporters. The *Kenosha News* published a portion of a *Time* magazine article, highlighting the "ragtag" supporters Wallace found in his Wisconsin campaign, including advocates of repealing the federal income tax and groups that wanted to "put more Christ into politics."[143] When arriving in Whitewater, a standing-room crowd of nearly two thousand was waiting to hear his speech, and he encountered a "Wallace for President" Club, led by junior Robert Peterson.[144] William Hable of Bloomer wrote to the editor of the *Eau Claire Daily Telegram* that it was not Wallace who was a carpetbagger but "northern lovemongers who go south as freedom riders."[145] He conceded that segregation was evil but argued that "forced integration was more evil," and African Americans would gain more rights without "violent emotional revisions of our constitutional concepts" caused by the overreaching Civil Rights Bill.[146]

An Alabamian, Cress Joiner, wrote to the *Milwaukee Journal* (which he blasted as left-wing press), praising Wallace as a great man "who wants to preserve our constitutional government."[147] Lance Lemphere wrote to the *Eau Claire Daily Telegram*, pointing out that both Wallace and Reynolds represented rotten factions of the party but conceded that Wallace was a "sincere and honest man."[148] Jim Parkinson told the *Green Bay Press-Gazette* that Wallace was right to question the bill, echoing the governor's concerns with private property and trial by jury rights eroding.[149] The *Wausau Daily Record-Herald* defended Wallace tepidly by arguing that he had the right to be heard and that Reynolds and other party leaders should challenge him head-on with a debate.[150]

THE FINAL STRETCH AND CRESCENDO AT SERB HALL

Wallace returned to Wisconsin on March 30, beginning a packed final week of his campaign. Wallace brushed aside personal criticisms and maintained the issue of states' rights was the focus of his campaign. In La Crosse, he rejected the idea that opposition to the Civil Rights Bill was a sectional issue, "but an issue of good men in the North and South who want to place the federal government back where it belongs."[151] Wallace warned that losing control over schools would be tantamount to the abolition of local government in La Crosse and Madison and wished to maintain "the form of government provided by the writers of the Constitution."[152]

Wallace continued "his now familiar speech" in Manitowoc, Sheboygan and Howards Grove on March 31, coupled with "truth kits" that were dispersed by the Wallace campaign with criticism of the Civil Rights Bill that they encouraged newspapers to publish.[153] He claimed that discrimination was not defined by the bill's authors, and he feared it would "destroy the Constitution of the United States."[154] Wallace again opposed the bill "not because it gave Negroes more rights, but because it would increase federal power."[155]

Wallace found his most raucous support (and some of his fiercest resistance) at an event on Milwaukee's south side Serb Hall on April 1, which Wallace claimed was "one of the best and most enthusiastic" crowds of his campaign.[156] The event started off with a verbal confrontation between Black protesters and the event's sponsor, south side tavern owner Bronko Gruber. When two Black protesters refused to stand for the national anthem, a racially charged shouting match ensued. There was preexisting tension between Polish and other ethnic white south siders and Milwaukee's Black community over integration and fair housing that contributed to this

Wallace signs autographs after his speech at Serb Hall. *AP photo/Charles Knoblock.*

eruption. Wallace remained out of the fray, and when he was introduced, he focused on federalism, not race. He received his loudest applause when he demanded the federal government "leave our affairs alone and let us run 'em ourselves!" At the end of his speech, he was "mobbed by autograph seekers" and supporters.[157]

As the campaign neared its conclusion, advertisements in local papers announced television engagements with increased frequency.[158] Despite CORE pickets, Wallace received a warm welcome at the Cuba Club in Madison, making "the same speech he made elsewhere."[159] The candidate claimed that while he didn't think Black people should face discrimination in hiring, he also didn't think employers "had to hire him because of [their race] either."[160] Wallace concluded his campaign with events at Marquette University on April 4 and with speeches in Kenosha and Racine on April 6.[161]

As media attention mounted the week before the election, so did protests against the governor. College students and religious leaders picketed the governor's events in La Crosse.[162] At Marquette University, 150 civil rights activists, nuns and priests picketed outside of the packed auditorium.[163] The *Milwaukee Sentinel* claimed that Wallace was "booed out of Wausau" by pupils after a brief event.[164] They wielded signs with messages including "States Rights or Human Rights" and "Wisconsin Doesn't Have Any Hate."[165]

Seventy-four Madison-area clergy signed a statement condemning Wallace's racism as "an insult to God and men."[166] Civil rights groups, particularly CORE and NAACP chapters in Milwaukee, began picketing events with dozens of vocal supporters.[167] In Kenosha, a picketer's sign struck Wallace as he left a speech.[168] Wallace's press secretary accused the picketers of being imported from Chicago and described the attempt to hit Wallace with a sign, which struck one of his security guards in the head. This attack garnered condemnation from the *Chicago Tribune*, which deemed the incident "unrepresentative behavior" and called on liberals and Wallace opponents to denounce the event.[169]

Attorney Bronson La Follette repudiated an Alabama paper's endorsement of Wallace that likened the governor to his grandfather, progressive champion "Fighting Bob" La Follette.[170] With less than a week before the campaign, President Johnson sent Postmaster General John Gronouski, a Polish American Wisconsinite, to the Badger State to rally support for Reynolds.[171] Republican strategists belatedly began planning more events for the Republican candidate, John Byrnes, to stave off perceptions that they were not doing enough in their own primary to reject Wallace's views.[172] Byrnes called on Republicans to not cross over in the open primary days before the campaign.[173] While he seemed sympathetic to Wallace's critique of an overly powerful central government diluting states' rights, Byrnes charged that governors like Wallace who "prostituted states' rights by using them to deny human freedom" necessitated federal power established in the Civil Rights Act.[174] The Republican claimed that his party represented freedom and opposed attempts to thwart it by both extending federal power unnecessarily and by stifling it "under the guise of states rights."[175] Even six-time socialist candidate Norman Thomas bashed Wallace at Ripon College, claiming his states' rights doctrine was "manifested in much brutality" in Alabama.[176]

The *La Crosse Tribune* criticized Wallace for "using" the Wisconsin primary as a referendum on civil rights and called on conservatives to abstain from supporting him.[177] Jack Hammond wrote to the *Eau Claire Daily Telegram* blasting Wallace as "a regressive element of democratic society that would prevent the blessings of liberty from being extended to all men."[178] The *Portage Daily Register* accused Wallace of casting a "dark cloud" of racial hatred over the state."[179] The *Catholic Herald* published an article with disparaging and offensive slurs in the title to highlight the hateful nature of Wallace's campaign.[180] The *Racine Journal-Times* implored readers to "vote for a Wisconsin man," either Reynolds or Byrnes.[181] Two days before the election, dozens of clergy and concerned Wisconsinites took out an ad in several Wisconsin papers denouncing Wallace and calling on them to vote for another candidate to ensure "equality before the law."[182] Wallace, for his part, responded with ads that included praise from religious leaders of Alabama, who defended his character and his opposition to the Civil Rights Bill, which one leader called a "calamity."[183]

Once again, in his last week, Wallace found supporters who welcomed his campaign on every stop. In La Crosse, the overflow audience of four hundred applauded Wallace and shouted down a student attempting to read a statement critical of the governor.[184] He also got generally positive ovations in Manitowoc and Sheboygan. The raucous support at Serb Hall shocked many in the

Wallace defending his record as Alabama governor in front of a Madison crowd. *From the* Capital Times, *photo by David Sandell; reprinted with permission.*

state, who began to predict Wallace having a large vote on Election Day.

"A Patriot" from West Allis blasted Reynolds for predicting support for Wallace from "extremists" in South Milwaukee, Mequon and Menominee Falls and argued that Wallace was a gentleman compared to Reynolds.[185] "For Wallace More Than Ever" slammed Reynolds for resorting to juvenile name-calling while praising Wallace "maintained a quiet dignity."[186]

WALLACE "WINS WITHOUT WINNING!"

When the votes were counted on election night, Wallace received 34 percent of the Democratic vote (25 percent of the total primary vote if one includes the Republican favorite son Byrnes), a shocking display that prompted a jubilant Wallace adorned in a Native American war bonnet to declare: "We won without winning!"[187] Reynolds won 66 percent of the Democratic candidates' vote (48 percent when Byrnes is included).

There are several theories about why Wallace won so many white votes in Wisconsin. Historian James Gregory argues that Wallace's success can be explained in the context of "northern backlash."[188] Gregory believes that the Wisconsin primary "echoed many of the instincts of blue collar whites who

Wallace celebrates his "win without winning" in Milwaukee, adorned with a Native American bonnet he was given by an indigenous Wisconsinite. *From the* La Crosse Tribune.

felt left behind by the changing agendas of northern liberalism,"[189] arguing that the southern governor played on the same class and racial divides in the North that were effective in Alabama. James T. Carter suggests several possible theories, including that right-wing Republicans crossed over in the open primary in the state (either to humiliate the party establishment or support Wallace's conservative views), there was a backlash of white blue-collar supporters who were marginalized by growing national forces and that suburban middle-class voters flocked to Wallace.[190] Carter wonders if voters truly favored Wallace's racism or if they were willing to look past his warts and embrace his small government ideals. Richard Haney argues that four factors best explain Wallace's support: public opposition to civil rights (particularly in Milwaukee neighborhoods), opposition to Governor Reynolds (who was unpopular because of his support of civil rights and other policies), crossover of Republican voters in the open primary and lack of organization on the part of the statewide Democratic Party.[191] Jody Carlson found that Wallace supporters were overwhelmingly white (99.1 percent) and opposed civil rights (85.8 percent), and this opposition was evenly distributed across most regions, including midwesterners (such as Wisconsinites), of whom 89.5 percent opposed civil rights legislation.[192]

While it is difficult to determine with any certainty which of these theories is correct, Wallace's use of states' rights rhetoric and defense of federalism explain his strength among conservatives in the Fox Valley, as well as his support on the south side of Milwaukee, where white ethnic voters were most fearful of open housing and integration. It was his use of this rhetoric, which had racial undertones without overt prejudice, that made his campaign shockingly successful in a progressive state.

SIGNIFICANCE

Despite his failure to win delegates in Wisconsin, Wallace replicated his showing in primaries in Indiana (where he won roughly the same percentage) and Maryland (where he racked up over 40 percent of the primary vote.[193] Ultimately, the Alabamian failed to win the party's nomination over incumbent Lyndon Johnson. Johnson's Republican opponent, Barry Goldwater, espoused conservative views and opposed civil rights legislation, and Wallace, content with his support in Wisconsin, Indiana and Maryland, withdrew from the race. "Today, we hear more states' rights talk than we have heard in the last quarter century," Wallace gloated in his concession speech. "I was the instrument through which this message was sent to the high counsels of both parties."[194] Yet despite his surprising success in the Wisconsin primary, Wallace was unable to prevent the passage of the Civil Rights Act. Overcoming a southern filibuster, the Senate passed the bill in June, and President Johnson signed the bill into law in July, less than three months after Wallace's "win" in Wisconsin.[195] Even though the Alabama governor could not prevent this assertion of federal authority over states and individuals, his rhetoric and campaign propelled him into a national figure as a proponent of states' rights and limited federal authority that would provide him more opportunities to "Stand up for America" and against civil rights in the not-so-distant future.

1964 WISCONSIN DEMOCRATIC PRIMARY

Civil Rights and Equal Protection

When George Wallace touched down in Milwaukee in 1964 to declare his candidacy for president, Wisconsin's Black population was nearly seventy-five thousand, a 600 percent increase from the 1940s. Many African Americans moved to Wisconsin to work in industrial jobs, mostly settling in the "inner core" of Milwaukee, which was emerging as one of the most racially segregated cities in the country. Black activists in Wisconsin were beginning to run into resistance on major civil rights issues, including school integration, fair housing and equal employment, and groups emerged to demonstrate and protest discrimination in the Badger State, often thought to be a bastion of liberal progressivism.[196] While Wallace viewed the battle lines through the prism of states' rights and federalism, Black activists believed a strong federal government was required to protect their constitutional rights. Correcting historical injustices meant calling for federal authority to guarantee African Americans' Fourteenth Amendment due process and equal protection rights, which had been denied for almost as long as they had been ratified.

In exploring mainstream newspapers, Black publications, and documents from local and national civil rights organizations from February through July 1964, one gains a clearer view on how African Americans reacted to Wallace's candidacy and electoral success by employing constitutional ideals and rhetoric. Resistance to the Wallace campaign in the Black community was seen through pickets and protests, publication of articles and cartoons, formation of alliances with other groups and electioneering. It is also clear that while Wallace was a concern to many people of color, he was not distracting community groups from other issues, including fair housing, school integration, hiring discrimination and the pending federal Civil Rights Bill. After Wallace's strong showing in the primary, African Americans criticized civil rights groups for not doing more to thwart the campaign, and many saw it as a wake-up call that confirmed larger racial problems in the oft-heralded progressive and liberal state.

PICKETS AND PROTEST

Members of the Black community in Wisconsin greeted Governor Wallace beginning at his first appearance in the Badger State in February through the April 7 primary election. Led by local chapters of the Congress of Racial Equality and the National Association for the Advancement of Colored People, Wallace's visits were met by peaceful but vocal protests, occasionally escalating into bellicose exchanges and confrontations. Even before Wallace declared his candidacy, the Madison chapters of CORE, NAACP and the Student Nonviolent Coordinating Committee (SNCC) picketed his February 19 speaking appearance. Thirty "placard-bearing pickets" greeted him with chants of "Jim Crow Must Go!" upon his arrival at the Madison Rotary Club, culminating with over two hundred picketers outside the Memorial Union. Additionally, during his speech, fifteen picketers walked out in silent protest.[197]

When Wallace flew back to Wisconsin to formally file papers to enter the race on March 7, his press conference was met with twenty-five CORE protesters picketing with signs reading "Wallace Blood is on Your Hands," a reference to the death of four girls who were killed in the bombing of a Birmingham church earlier that year.[198] On March 16, as Wallace kicked off his campaign in Appleton, the *Milwaukee Journal* reported that a Wallace backer, Roy A. Jones, "received 40 to 45 threatening phone calls," and "a number of unidentified Negroes demonstrated in front of [Jones's] house," leading Wallace to criticize the protesters for violating the "sanctity of the home."[199] This quip prompted Tuskegee Institute instructor Elizabeth Keen to write a letter to the editor, published on March 25, calling out Wallace's hypocrisy, noting that "'the sanctity of home' is not a phrase that one can apply to Negro homes in Birmingham, where more than 40 bombings still remain unsolved, and elsewhere in Alabama."[200]

Despite Wallace's heckling of protesters, their frequency and numbers grew as Wallace's campaign gained increasingly larger audiences and media attention. At an event in Oshkosh, "thirty-four signs were raised in opposition to Wallace, and only four in his support," with messages that included "'No Police Dogs in Oshkosh', and 'Welcome Hatemongers.'"[201] When students at Oshkosh State College gave Wallace the thumbs-down signal, refused to shake his hand, surrounded his car and started singing "We Shall Overcome," Wallace quipped, "Don't you know 'Home on the Range?'"[202] During a protest in Whitewater, with students wielding signs with messages including "Don't Tolerate Intolerance," Wallace "carefully sought out and shook hands of the only two Negroes in sight,"[203] in an apparent attempt to demonstrate his opposition to the Civil Rights Bill was an issue of federalism, not prejudice. One of the Black students requested Wallace's autograph, but unbeknownst to the candidate, he signed a copy of the Civil Rights Bill he so adamantly opposed.[204]

One of the more successful demonstrations happened the next day at St. Norbert College in De Pere. Protesters, singing "Swing Low Sweet Chariot,"[205] distributed handouts, encouraging audience members to neither applaud nor stoop to his level by getting disorderly but instead to remember that "Silence is Golden."[206] Apparently, this silence unnerved Wallace, marking "the only time during the primary that Wallace lost his platform composure."[207] During a question-and-answer session, a Black student from Milwaukee named Thomas Holton asked Wallace, "Are Negroes Human Beings?" Two papers wrote that Wallace quietly replied yes,[208] and one paper quoted him as saying, "I believe God created all of us."[209] Holton then asked defiantly, "Well then why don't you treat them like they are?"[210] Wallace deflected, advising "the students to take a good look at conditions on Indian reservations in Wisconsin before being too harsh on Alabama."[211] This reference to tensions between Native and white Americans, who were clashing over tribal sovereignty and rights in Wisconsin, was meant to point out hypocrisy of northern critics of Wallace's segregationist policies.

On the same day as the event at St. Norbert's, the Milwaukee CORE chapter and the state and local chapters of the NAACP announced an anti-Wallace march on Wisconsin Avenue in Milwaukee.[212] A CORE flyer for the event called on people to fight Wallace's "racist, segregationist policies," indicating "Milwaukee does not welcome a man with blood of four innocent Negro children on his hands."[213] Leaders announced the event in the *Milwaukee Sentinel* and a Black newspaper, the *Milwaukee Star*. An article in the *Star* calls on "indignant citizens" to join the march and "show [Wallace]

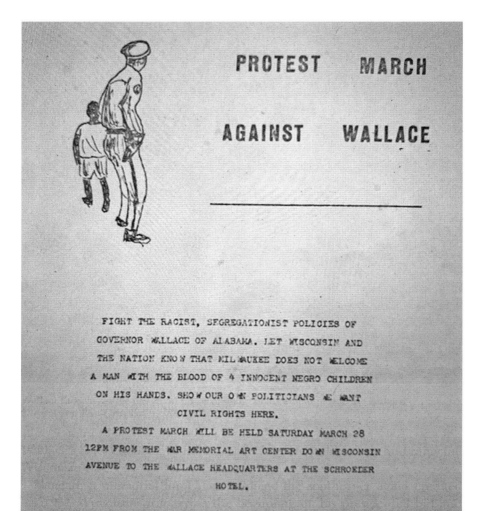

Milwaukee's CORE chapter tried to defeat Wallace in a variety of ways, including holding a rally, as this flyer indicates. *Wisconsin Historical Society, Core Records, Milwaukee MSS 27, Box 1 Folder 7.*

the people of Wisconsin don't want him."[214] The article also describes a campaign by Milwaukee's CORE chapter's call-in "to register protest against his entry" into the primary, which kept the "switchboards busy throughout the afternoon and evening."[215] The *Racine Journal-Times* reported the event as 175 marchers strong; the throng took forty minutes to walk the mile from the Memorial Center to the Schroeder Hotel, touting signs that said Wallace was "rotten to the CORE."[216]

The most racially charged event in Wallace's Wisconsin campaign happened on April 1 at Serb Hall on the south side of Milwaukee. Despite eighty-five picketers from eight civil rights groups outside the event, a crowd of 350 people inside gave Wallace "a boisterous endorsement" and "one of the most enthusiastic receptions…since he started campaigning."[217] The predominantly Polish, Serb and eastern European south siders rose to a fever pitch when event organizer and bar owner Bronko Gruber "pointed out two Negro men who had remained seated during the singing of the National Anthem."[218] Boos and a shout of "Send them back to Africa!" from white audience members led to jeers from Black attendees, many of whom were patrons of Gruber's bar.[219] The two men eventually left, but a Black Baptist minister, Reverend Leo R. Champion, began shouting, "Get your dogs out!" to Gruber.[220] As an audience member shoved a Wallace sign in the reverend's face, Gruber claimed that Black men in his neighborhood assaulted his friends and old ladies and raped women. When Gruber asked, "Did I fight at Guadalcanal and come back for this?" someone in the audience shouted back, "They fought beside you!"[221] Gruber denied having ever seen a Black man in combat before returning to his introduction of Wallace. When Wallace took the stage, the remaining Black audience members walked out, and Wallace went on to give his speech. When the speech ended, he escaped out the back door to avoid the remaining picketers.[222]

Despite the electric and combative scene at Serb Hall, Black activists were undeterred. Madison CORE members protested outside a speech at the Cuba Club "in the driving rain," singing songs and marching in opposition to Wallace.[223] On April 4, over 150 pickets outside of Marquette University (about one-third of which were thought to be members of Milwaukee civil rights groups) forced police to shut down Wisconsin Avenue. A Black assemblyman named Isaac Coggs was not allowed entry, and adding to the chaos, a bomb threat was made—it was ultimately a hoax.[224] Protesters banged on the locked auditorium doors, interrupting Wallace's speech several times, and one CORE member, dressed in a Klan outfit, carried a

Two Black protesters refuse to stand during the national anthem at a Wallace rally at Serb Hall, sparking a confrontation with his supporters. *From the* Capital Times, *reprinted with permission.*

Members of Madison's CORE chapter picket a Wallace speech outside the Cuba Club in the pouring rain. *From the* Capital Times, *reprinted with permission.*

sign reading, "Lynch Discrimination."[225] There was chanting and shouting at Wallace's car as he left, and one person "hurled a clod of dirt, grass and gravel…striking the side of the car" but did no damage.[226] The *Milwaukee Star* described the protesters, including minister Leo Champion, as marching with "orderly chaos," having "noses red, eyes watering from the cold," and chanting "two, four, six, eight, we don't want to segregate!" and "one, three, five, nine, I'll take freedom anytime!"[227] The next day in Kenosha, police arrested a white protester in a crowd of over 75 pickets for apparently striking Wallace with a sign. The NAACP and CORE were active in the event, with members holding signs saying, "We're for Rights, Not Racism.[228] According to the *Milwaukee Journal*, the young crowd was half Black, and protesters were "having a good time" chanting and singing Beatles melodies with the words changed to "We hate Wallace."[229] CORE leaders described the pickets as "a moral victory" and "an experience and a lesson most people who viewed it won't forget."[230]

The Black community marched, spoke out, held events and challenged Governor Wallace on nearly every campaign stop. Their attempts to disrupt the campaign might have been unsuccessful, but they refused to allow Wallace to brush off his racist record as a simple states' rights issue.

A Little (Sometimes Very Little) Help from Their Friends

While a surprising number of white voters would ultimately cast ballots for an avowed racist and segregationist, many allies joined Black activists in opposing the Wallace candidacy. Wallace attacked the press throughout the campaign, arguing that papers like the *Milwaukee Journal* and *Milwaukee Sentinel*, which he called the "left-wing press," were covering his views and candidacy unfairly, particularly noting that some political cartoons were "downright cruel."[231] Wallace's press secretary, Bill Jones, criticized the *Milwaukee Journal*, among other papers, for focusing more on the "beatniks" and pickets more than the substance of Wallace's speeches, arguing that the papers lacked journalistic integrity by editorializing rather than being objective.[232] In examining the coverage in mainstream papers, it is apparent that they did cover, to varying degrees, protests, jeers and critical opposition to Wallace, but there were ample examples of letters to the editor that were pro-Wallace and most stories appeared relatively neutral and fact-based. Wallace certainly sought out media attention, holding press conferences

The press was critical of Wallace's candidacy, as seen in this cartoon in the *Capital Times*. *From the* Capital Times, *reprinted with permission.*

and public events throughout his campaign, and the press was happy to oblige by covering the circus-like atmosphere.

While the press may have occasionally given voice to Wallace's opposition, many religious leaders were more steadfast allies to the cause. The *Catholic Herald*, a publication of the Milwaukee and Madison dioceses, contained an editorial by theology professor Father John T. O'Connor, condemning Wallace as a "moral evil…invading Wisconsin."[233] O'Connor stated that a Catholic could not vote for an avowed segregationist, and Wallace was "publicly known for promoting that type of racism which has been specifically condemned by Pope Pius XI."[234] Skeptical Protestant ministers in Oshkosh also grilled Wallace, asking pointed questions about his segregationist beliefs.[235] Catholic priests, nuns and seminarians even joined the picket line at Wallace's speech on Marquette's campus,[236] and a group of Protestant clergymen (including three Black ministers) and a rabbi issued a statement following a Kenosha event decrying the governor for denying Alabamians "the full sweep of their rights and opportunities as citizens and children of God, equal in his sight."[237] On April 1, Black priest Father John LaBauve addressed five hundred women at the Edgewood College of Madison Diocesan Council of Catholic Women, praising the Black activists for "rejecting paternalism" in fighting for unalienable rights which they had "purchased with their own blood" through war service and sacrifice.[238] Without naming Wallace, he criticized his campaign as attempting to "propagate his Southern way of life."[239] There is ample evidence that many people of faith saw Wallace's values as incongruent with their beliefs, and they spoke out in unison with Black activists to oppose his candidacy.

There was also evidence of many white supporters who protested, picketed and challenged Wallace at his events, in particular outside of Milwaukee and Madison, where few Black residents lived. Over one hundred protesters wearing armbands met Wallace in Chippewa Falls on March 28, but he evaded the orderly marchers by entering through the back door.[240] On April 1, students in Sheboygan and Howards Grove carried anti-Wallace signs and "blackened their faces in protest against Wallace's segregationist policies."[241] While students in these places were almost exclusively white (one paper noted that there was "only one Negro family in the Fox River Valley,"[242]

In a gesture that would now be seen as racially insensitive, white students in rural Sheboygan County blackened their faces to show support for civil rights in Wisconsin at an anti-Wallace demonstration. *AP photo.*

No Explosion if Everyone
Votes His Conscience

This cartoon in the *Wisconsin State Journal* warned voters to take Wallace's candidacy seriously. *From the* Wisconsin State Journal, *reprinted with permission.*

where Wallace kicked off his campaign), Wallace met people who opposed his racist and segregationist policies at every stop.

Other groups were also quick to ally themselves with the Black activists for different reasons and to varying degrees. Labor leaders, including AFL-CIO president George Haberman and Wisconsin Committee on Political Education president John Schmidt, were wary of Wallace's right-to-work track record and opposed Wallace but were not particularly focused on his record on civil rights.[243] Liberal and progressive elected officials in the state rallied behind favorite son candidate Governor John Reynolds, blasting Wallace's racist views. Reynolds campaigned on behalf of Johnson using brutal imagery from Birmingham on campaign materials, actively promoting the pending civil rights legislation and imploring supporters in a campaign speech to go to "Vicksburg in Mississippi and visit the cemetery there and see the graves of Wisconsin men who died because they believed in the equality of man."[244] But the Democratic Party itself did very little in the way of funding the campaign, and there was little coordination with civil rights groups.[245] Faculty on university campuses also opposed Wallace, with one professor at the University of Wisconsin–Milwaukee blasting his campaign as "concentrated, demagogic advertising" and another fearful that Wallace's support of segregation was a "great danger to the democratic foundation of the entire country."[246] While support from outside groups was present, it varied in its strength and voracity.

THE IMPORTANCE OF THE BLACK PRESS

The Wallace campaign also generated a widespread and notable reaction not just on the picket lines but also in the Black press. Discussion and criticism of Wallace's campaign began to appear in a number of regional sources by February 1, 1964, ranging from critical articles, satirical mockery, press releases from national organizations and scathing political cartoons. These sources give more substantive and specific concerns and criticism from the Black community than the mainstream press was willing to cover.

In 1964, the primary newspaper serving the Black community in Milwaukee was the *Milwaukee Star.* The paper covered broad topics of interest in the days surrounding Wallace's campaign, ranging from news and activism around a number of social issues, high school city sports, church life, "Outdoors in Wisconsin," women's style and fashion, arts and culture, teen news and a spirited opinion and letters to the editors page. Wallace first appeared on the front page on February 22 in a folksy article titled, "Southern Governor Ducks Civil Rights Welcome." The author calls Wallace "the little man with the big mouth" who "was talkin' hard, but he was walkin' soft as he slipped in and out of back doors to dodge Wisconsin picketing."[247] The author described the protesters as "well-integrated, unafraid and healthy—or at least strong-voiced Northern-style demonstrators" from CORE, NAACP, Young Christian Workers and "ornery independents" encountering hostile Wallace supporters telling them to go "back where they came from (Africa)."[248] There was also description of a "freedom relay" in coordination with two hundred Madison activists. The article did concede, however, that there was "some truth" to Wallace's criticism of de facto segregation in the North.[249]

The *Star* next mentioned Wallace in its March 21 edition. The candidate gained significantly more coverage as his campaign gained momentum. In an article titled "Wallace Picks Wis," the author noted that Wallace was "more at home in Wisconsin than he is in Alabama," appealing to conservatives with his rhetoric on "states rights, property rights, and individual rights (if the individual happens to be an Anglo-Saxon employer or his pink cheeked child)."[250] The author argued that Wallace tapped into Wisconsin's preexisting "white power structure that 'adjusts' sufficiently to the 'Northern liberal' image to fool even itself," noting with disappointment that northern white "Santa Clauses" pretend to support African Americans but "never pass out the goodies of FEP laws, open housing, or equal education."[251] The author hopes that Wallace's campaign will awake "militant Negroes" in Wisconsin out of passivity and precipitate a change in white Wisconsinites who "won't like the sound" of their prejudice-laden support of Wallace.[252] Editor Larry Saunders blasted "the governor of a police state" in his opinion piece, referring to his candidacy as an "insult to the state of Wisconsin and its' citizens."[253] Saunders implored readers to take his candidacy seriously, however, and vote against "the carrier of hate, a nonbeliever of all things that go to make up a democracy."[254] Wallace is also mentioned in reporter Jeffrey Kay's news piece about John Howard Griffin, author of *Black Like Me*, a book about a white man who darkened his face to examine life in the segregated South. Griffin criticizes Wallace's tepid efforts at bringing the murderers of the four girls in Birmingham to justice, assigning him blame for establishing "the climate of hatred which permitted the bombing."[255] Griffin predicted that if Wallace were to have success in Wisconsin, it would be because "good men remained silent."[256] Finally, in "Alabamians Say Wallace Hurts State and U.S.," freelance journalist William Bradford Huie accused Wallace of inciting the racially motivated violence in his state.[257]

The *Star* provided its final indictment of Wallace in its election eve issue. It endorsed a number of Black candidates, as well as either Governor Reynolds or the Republican candidate, Representative John Byrnes, "urging all Milwaukeeans of integrity to remain true to the party of their choice in voting for one of the favorite sons."[258] The paper also featured a lengthy interview with Huie (who was on a Wisconsin "hell-raising tour against Wallace"), in which he accused Wallace of having a mental disability as well as connections to the Ku Klux Klan.[259]

Black newspapers also used political cartoons to good effect. A cartoon titled "The Old Story: The Art of Subterfuge" showed a shifty-looking George Wallace cowardly sneaking out the back door as picketers demand "Wallace Must Go!" and "Equality Now!"[260] Another cartoon titled "Setting the Pace for Wallace?" portrayed Democratic Milwaukee mayor Henry Maier, who was regularly criticized in the *Star* as being unsympathetic to civil rights concerns such as school integration and housing, wearing a hat with a Confederate flag standing next to a road block labeled "civil rights progress" and holding a traffic sign saying, "Go Slow, Y'all." The mayor is blocking a Black runner labeled "Milw. 1964."[261] The implication of the cartoon is that while Wallace preached overt segregation and was an avowed racist, northern liberals like Maier covertly raised obstacles to success in the Black community. These cartoons effectively expressed criticism by Black activists during the campaign in a humorous way.

In addition to local coverage in the *Milwaukee Star*, the *Chicago Defender* picked up a number of stories on the campaign, signaling there was notable regional awareness of and attention on the divisive candidate in the Black community. On March 10, a wire article announced Wallace's decision to file for president in Wisconsin, noting he was "expected to campaign…on a platform of states' rights" while avoiding "the race issue."[262] A March 18 article chronicled the beginning of his campaign in Appleton, the home of former senator Joseph McCarthy, whom Wallace praised as decent man "who gave good warnings of left wingers and communists."[263] On April 2, the *Defender* picked up a story of Wisconsin Democratic senator William

Cartoons in the *Milwaukee Star* criticize the Wallace campaign and northern liberals who stand in the way of civil rights. Provided by the *Milwaukee Courier*.

Proxmire's claim that "a vote for Wallace is a vote for bigotry that provoked the terrible church bombing that took the lives of four little innocent Negro girls."[264] The paper also focused on the "first violent event" of the campaign in Kenosha, when the governor was "clipped in the side of the head by a cardboard sign wielded by demonstrators.[265] Unlike the mainstream Milwaukee papers, the *Defender* named local CORE chairman Walter Vaughn as the organizer of the event, and characterized the "flying fists" and "heavy rain for more than two hours" in a more dramatic way that focused on the protesters' point of view.[266] In addition to the *Defender*, *Jet Magazine* featured two photos of Wallace protesters and an article about the Catholic clergy's denunciation of the campaign in two April editions.[267]

Finally, the executive secretary of the NAACP, Roy Wilkins, sent a letter to all of the major Wisconsin daily newspapers in Appleton, Beloit, Eau Claire, Fond du Lac, Green Bay, Janesville, Jefferson County, Kenosha, La Crosse, Madison, Manitowoc, Milwaukee, Oshkosh, Racine, Sheboygan, Superior, Waukesha and Wausau. He warned that voting for Wallace would be "interpreted by the nation and the world as endorsements of the Alabamian's racism," and he chronicled Wallace's track record of prejudice as governor and judge. He rejected Wallace's federalism states' rights argument and implored Wisconsinites to exercise "their well-known individuality and independence" in rejecting Wallace's candidacy.[268] Finally, Wilkins warned,

> *Wisconsin citizens must surely know that while an individual man is free to cherish racial spite as a personal matter, a governmental policy of keeping the foot on the neck of a man or a people cannot stand among the descendants of men who threw off the boot of George III off the neck of the thirteen colonies. After all, the next neck chosen by the Wallaces of this era may not be black.[269]*

While it is not clear what effect these articles and cartoons had on the larger Black community, they demonstrate a level of activism, awareness and dialogue around Wallace's campaign that was prevalent from February to April 1964.

GET OUT THE (BLACK) VOTE!

In addition to opposing Wallace actively, there is evidence that Black activists were electioneering to defeat him as well as elect their own Black candidates. An article in the *Milwaukee Star* summarizes a press release from Black alderperson Vel Phillips, reminding residents of an upcoming voter registration deadline.[270] The March 14 *Star* promoted "a fully-manned nonpartisan voter registration center" with twenty-one phone lines, ten drivers and babysitters to eliminate obstacles to voter registration.[271] The next week, Clinton Rose, director of the electioneering, deemed the effort a success, having made over thirty-one thousand phone calls, with fewer than one hundred of those contacted not planning to register and over one hundred transportation requests for registration.[272] In its April 4 edition, the *Star* endorsed candidates, particularly community-level candidates of color; promoted free rides to the polls offered by the Northside Tavern Keepers Association; and provided information about wards, districts and candidate platforms.[273] There is ample evidence that the Black community was not just reacting to Wallace's toxic campaign but proactively running for office, promoting candidates and providing get-out-the vote efforts to build electoral agency.

Bigger than Wallace

In spite of the media circus that surrounded Wallace's campaign and the organized response by the Black community, evidence reveals that reacting to the Alabama governor was not the only, or even the primary, goal of Black activists at the time. While the response to Wallace mattered, it did not distract civil rights groups from other more longstanding and pressing issues in Wisconsin.

Examination of the Black and mainstream presses sheds light on a wide variety of goals and initiatives Black activists were working on that were unrelated to the Wallace campaign. The March 1 edition of the *Oshkosh Northwestern* featured a photo of the chairman of the United Milwaukee Council on Human Rights, Theodore Mack, pointing a finger at Governor Reynolds, demanding that he appoint an African American to a county judgeship or risk losing support from the Black community.[274] CORE members from Illinois and Wisconsin met in Chicago on March 7, reasserting their commitment to "nonviolent, direct action" by civil rights groups, even if the pending Civil Rights Bill passed, noting that enforcement might be inconsistent pending court appeals.[275] This conference laid out areas in which African Americans and "sympathetic whites…form a mass movement for political pressure, including housing, employment and education."[276] On March 10, Milwaukee CORE chairman John Givens publicly criticized the Milwaukee-based company Allen-Bradley for "an obvious dodge" in its failure to address its lack of employment of African Americans. The article also noted that earlier the Negro American Labor Council's (NALC) Milwaukee chapter filed a complaint of racial discrimination.[277] The *Milwaukee Star* quoted NALC president Calvin T. Sherard's letter to the federal Equal Employment Opportunity Committee criticizing Allen-Bradley as being a "symbol of racial discrimination," since it employed only "four negroes out of six thousand employees."[278] Madison's CORE chapter followed suit by picketing outside Sears-Roebuck on March 25, which the *Wisconsin State Journal* condemned as "accomplishing nothing but ill will."[279] Interestingly, the unsigned editorial suggests that CORE, which was mostly college students, went ahead with the protest in spite of opposition from the Madison NAACP (which the paper claimed was predominantly residents "who are more interested in solving problems than in having fun protesting them"[280]) who reportedly recommended first going to the EEOC with actual evidence of discrimination.[281]

Days after the election, CORE protested housing discrimination at the Milwaukee Home Show, with picketers carrying signs and balloons in the arena. Givens criticized realtors as being "the strongest forces against open occupancy."[282] The article cited an experiment initiated by the group that revealed Black members who applied for apartments were given a higher rent price than white members who applied a half hour earlier.[283] CORE also awarded two Milwaukeeans, Dr. James Barnett and Helen Barnhill, for "courageous work in advancing the concept of equality of opportunity in housing" at a housing conference in Springfield Illinois.[284] Additionally, the Milwaukee Urban league battled unemployment and underemployment of Black residents by establishing a "skills bank" to help them connect to jobs in the region.[285]

Education was a primary area of concern for Milwaukee civil rights groups during Wallace's campaign. School integration was the major focus of the *Milwaukee Star* for much of the time Wallace was campaigning, and divisions in the Black community and the Milwaukee public school board spilled over into the mainstream press. NAACP state president Lloyd Barbee and other education representatives of CORE began calling for "'specific requests' for desegregating Milwaukee schools"[286] as early as February 22, confronting the school board–established special committee for equality of educational opportunity, led by Harold Story. Activists, clergy and community members held a meeting on March 1, calling for a withdrawal of inner core schools as a protest against the board's slow integration and busing policies, proposing seven ways to integrate more effectively public schools.[287] This led E'Allyne Perkins, president of the Milwaukee council of the National Council of Negro Women to criticize the NAACP and CORE in an open letter summarized in the *Milwaukee Journal*. Perkins argued the boycott would be counterproductive, urging civil rights leaders to give the board's committee more time to find solutions and urging cooperation.[288] Barbee and others were undeterred and formed the Milwaukee United School Integration Committee (MUSIC), meeting with ministers, touring schools in the city that had antiquated textbooks and used paddles to discipline Black children and railing against "token integration" and the glacial progress of the superintendent and school board."[289] While the Black paper focused on the goals and actions of the civil rights groups, the mainstream papers focused on Black anti-boycott groups and published cartoons critical of the usefulness of the protests.[290]

Black activists also welcomed a number of high-profile national leaders to Wisconsin during this window to help further their civil rights goals.

For example, Martin Luther King visited Milwaukee, criticizing de facto segregation and calling for action in the community. June Shagaloff from the national NAACP education office came to Milwaukee to work with MUSIC, as did comedian and activist Dick Gregory.[291] While Wallace was clearly of concern to the Black community, they also kept their eyes on the prize, working to create a fairer and more equitable community rather than obsessing over a racist outsider.

THE BLACK COMMUNITY'S REACTION TO WALLACE'S "WIN"

While there has been much written about how to explain the motivations of white voters who cast their ballots for Wallace, there is little about how their Black neighbors interpreted and reacted to 25 percent of Wisconsin voters supporting an archetype of the Jim Crow South. Some tried to put a positive spin on the results (75 percent of Wisconsinites did *not* vote for him after all), while others found them disheartening. Many Black Wisconsinites were critical of organizations like the NAACP and CORE, arguing they sat on their hands and should have done more to defeat Wallace more soundly. Many saw the results as a wake-up call and tried to use them as a springboard to greater electoral and community engagement. For others, the results were unsurprising and confirmed that Wisconsin was not the land of milk and honey that many northern liberals imagined.

One Wisconsinite wrote a letter to NAACP executive director Roy Wilkins, claiming that despite the fact that he despised Wallace and supported civil rights legislation, he voted for Wallace "because he despised our present governor of Wisconsin [Reynolds] even more." He claimed that every person he talked to who voted for Wallace did the same thing."[292] Indeed, even as President Johnson won 62 percent of Wisconsin's vote in the general election, Reynolds would lose the gubernatorial race, winning roughly the same percentage he carried in the presidential primary. In his correspondence back to the Sturgeon Bay resident, Wilkins stated that be believed "the majority of the votes cast in Wisconsin could not necessarily be counted as a vote for Wallace" and analysis was needed to see what factors led to such protest votes."[293]

There was criticism in the Black community that leaders like Wilkins should have done more to fight the mistruths of the Wallace campaign. Charles J.

While most were surprised by Wallace's strong showing, this cartoon expresses the worry that Wallace might garner significant support. *From the* Capital Times, *reprinted with permission.*

Livingston of the *Associate Negro Press* wrote a scathing critique of leaders of the NAACP, CORE and SNCC, claiming they were "mute on how best to fight Wallace's determination to continue to exploit the fears and prejudices of white Northerners," arguing that leaders of these groups "were strangely silent as to what plans they had, if any, to counteract Wallace's campaign of distortion, 'falsehoods,' and innuendoes."[294] Livingston believed the groups lacked a "coordinated or comprehensive plan to fight the hate campaign and efforts to scuttle the rights bill" and vented frustrations that "young civil rights militants, meanwhile were asking: 'Why do we always let the racists grab a big lead before we doing [*sic*] anything? Why don't our leaders and politicians show more foresight?"[295] In fact, in a brief Western Union telegram from Wilkins to Madison NAACP president Marshall Colston, the national chief expressed regret that he was "unable to aid financially in campaign you outlined on April 7 Primary. [I] Suggest Wisconsin branches picket Wallace rallies."[296] More could have and should have been done, many Black activists believed.

Most activists did not use the defeat as an opportunity to attack their own, however, but to call for more united action on community-based and electoral organizing. An unnamed African American interviewed by the *Milwaukee Sentinel* on April 19 said the results would "shock complacent liberals and move some Negroes to more civil rights activity."[297] Edward Smyth, president of the Milwaukee branch of the NAACP, said he was glad for the vote because he hoped it would awaken Black people who had been brainwashed by "good white friends" and encourage them to "realize the impact of the ballot" going forward.[298] Lillian Calhoun, who had a regular column on civil rights topics in the *Daily Defender*, also saw the Wallace vote as a call to organize, stating,

> *Too often we let a lot of intellectual gobblegood* [sic] *blind us to political power. That's all we've got, folks. So you'd better make use of it. Work in the primaries, work in your ward organizations, work in the elections.*[299]

For other Black activists, Wallace's success only confirmed what was already self-evident to them: Wisconsin was a place with racial prejudice not dissimilar to Alabama. On election night, Milwaukee's CORE chairman John Givens Jr. argued the vote was much bigger than Wallace and was the result of "a deep-seated thing in Milwaukee for a long time."[300] Alderperson Vel Phillips, who won her race the same night as Wallace's "win," stated,

> *Many good Wisconsin citizens have conditioned themselves to the safe, sound thought that we in Wisconsin are progressive liberals and don't need demonstrations. I think this will certainly awaken them to the fact that we do need demonstrations.*[301]

Reverend Louis S. Beauchamp, president of the Wisconsin General Baptist Conference, found solace in the results, since it confirmed "what we've been talking about. We don't have to say [prejudice] is here. The whole state now knows it's here."[302] Milwaukee NAACP head Edward Smyth saw the Wallace vote as a "chance for [white voters] to get their licks in," if they felt threatened by school integration, job stability, occupancy and housing legislation or the Civil Rights Bill.[303] Lloyd Barbee worried that in the absence of more vocal support of African Americans' rights, Wisconsin was vulnerable to its own "homegrown demagogue."[304]

The *Milwaukee Star* echoed much of the frustration of Black civil rights leaders but had an optimistic view of a path forward. While touting three victories by Black candidates (a record at the time), the paper characterized Wallace's symbolic win as a setback for the pending Civil Rights Bill that "changes the face of Wisconsin in the eyes of the world."[305] While one Black supervisor, Calvin Moody, said he had heard some Black people had voted for the Alabamian, Vel Phillips said she "knew no Negroes so uninformed that he would vote for Wallace."[306] An unsigned article wondered what Black activists could learn from Wallace himself, half admiringly praising his complete commitment to his cause (even if it was a terrible one), his calm composure in the face of opposition, his determination to find victory in spite of winning no delegates, his expertise in "civil wrongs" and how to communicate his views to the populace.[307] The author questioned "fence-sitting when it comes to human rights" and called on activists to learn to adapt Wallace's tactics to win victories on integrated education, open housing and fair employment practices.[308] An editorial by Larry Saunders lamented the difficulty in telling the "difference between democracy and a slave state" and questioned who could be trusted after nearly a quarter of a million votes were cast for Wallace. He called on Black community members to band together, promoted voter education efforts and implored readers to "be counted" at the polls.[309] Over the next few issues, there were fleeting references to Wallace in the *Star*. Visitors to Milwaukee like NAACP education assistant June Shagaloff claimed that broad conclusions of Wallace's strong performance amounted to "unjustified interpretations,"[310] and Dick Gregory called Wallace "dumb" and said that Wisconsin was "just as rotten" as his southern home.[311]

The *Milwaukee Star* also published two political cartoons in the aftermath of Wallace's surprising showing, both notable for having violent undertones. One depicts Wallace as a chicken, strutting after fooling a quarter of Wisconsin voters, while a Black man with an axe (labeled "direct action"), says, "Yeah baby, but you don't fool ME!"[312] A week later, another featured a Black man drawn discarding a hatchet labeled 25 percent (the number of Wallace voters) and using a larger hatchet labeled "75% Wis. Vote" (The number that voted against Wallace) to cut through a jungle of Dixiecrat opposition on a "rough civil rights trail."[313] These cartoons demonstrate

Cartoons from the *Milwaukee Star* strike a violent but activist tone in moving beyond Wallace's "win" and uniting to bring about meaningful change. *Provided by* Milwaukee Courier *newspaper.*

the desire of activists to empower themselves by using the Wallace vote as springboard to stronger and more united opposition to discrimination.

Another Black newspaper, the *Milwaukee Courier*, formed a few months after Wallace's run. While it missed the day-to-day of the campaign, the July 3 issue featured a piece by a Milwaukee psychologist who applied a logic test to conclude that supporters of Wallace may have believed the logic of his states' rights, anti-civil rights campaign, but "what he says does not conform with the evidence" and "the civil rights bill does not do what he says it will, and he is not against civil rights for the reasons he gives."[314] This psychoanalysis of Wallace was unique to other perspectives and criticisms of Wallace by the Black community.

While it is clear that activists in the Black community responded to Wallace's campaign in a variety of ways, it is worth noting that examining newspapers and rhetoric at rallies does not necessarily reveal what average people of color thought or did. These accounts, while revealing, lack street-level agency of ordinary citizens, and one cannot assume that all African Americans were aware of or had strong feelings about Wallace based on the actions of a core group of activists.

SIGNIFICANCE

African Americans in Wisconsin were tested in the crucible of the 1964 primary election and emerged more united to take on the injustice around them. While Wallace's campaign caused none of these problems, his presence brought these divisions and issues to the forefront in Wisconsin and altered the course of these debates in an important and enduring way.

Empowering themselves with constitutional arguments, activists demanded that their equal protection rights be guaranteed by federal authorities. Wallace's campaign and electoral success demonstrated the necessity of the goals and movement. With an alarming number of fellow Wisconsinites embracing what activists saw as a demagogic and racist campaign camouflaged under the guise of states' rights, activists sought to embarrass Wallace and thwart his candidacy to protect the pending federal Civil Rights Bill and achieve tangible gains in the Badger State. While they could not prevent Wallace from "winning" in Wisconsin, his success did not prevent the passage of the landmark Civil Rights Act of 1964 months later, ensuring federal protection for Black Wisconsinites by outlawing discrimination based on race or color. There would be more federal victories in the years to come as well as more encounters with Wallace and his Wisconsinite supporters.

1968 PRESIDENTIAL CAMPAIGN

Stand Up for Wisconsin! Wallace and Milwaukee Civil Rights on the National Stage

Wallace Becomes a National Candidate

Following his failed primary run, George Wallace faced another impending crisis in Selma, Alabama. Dr. King and his group, the Southern Christian Leadership Conference, planned a fifty-mile march from Selma to Montgomery to demand voting rights for African Americans, which were nearly nonexistent in Alabama. The governor refused to concede to the protesters, retorting that he was "not going to have a bunch of n——— walking along the highway in this state as long as I'm governor."[315] As the group tried to cross the Edmund Pettus Bridge, troopers led by Sheriff Jim Clark attacked them with gas and clubs, and it was captured on television and viewed by a national audience.[316]

While criticism for the state's role in fostering a culture of violence and hatred was widespread, Wallace did not take responsibility for the events on the Edmund Pettus Bridge. While Wallace claimed he wanted to avoid violence, he defended the troopers' actions as justified, protecting the marchers from antagonists waiting on the other side.[317]

Still, after Bloody Sunday and the murder of Reverend James Reeb, Wallace attempted to avoid damaging national perceptions that might tank his run for president in 1968 by coming to Washington to meet with President Johnson, his primary opponent four years earlier. Johnson, using his forcefully persuasive techniques in the private meeting, overpowered Wallace's feeble attempts at arguing for states' rights to protect citizens without federal involvement. Johnson blasted Wallace for allowing such violence under his watch and chastised the governor for his refusal to do more to register Black voters. When Wallace claimed he was powerless to compel state registrars, Johnson snapped, "Don't shit me about your persuasive power....I was watching you on the television [this morning]... and you were attacking me."[318] Wallace countered that his gripes were not with the president personally but federal intervention in general. Johnson was unconvinced, lampooning the governor for his failure to guarantee and protect his Black citizens' voting rights. When the meeting ended, both men left the room and held a brief press conference. Johnson threw no punches, flatly stating that Wallace needed to do more to support voting rights and condemn violence against the protesters. Then, he dropped a huge announcement, with Wallace standing right next to him: the president would be proposing a sweeping voting rights bill to Congress in two days that would address the inequities in Alabama and around the South. When it was Wallace's turn to address the media, he was speechless.[319] A couple of years earlier, Wallace's Stand in the Schoolhouse Door opened the door for the Civil Rights Act; now Bloody Sunday paved the way for the Voting Rights Act. The states' rights–minded governor's actions or inaction had prompted sweeping federal actions.

In 1966, Alabama law prohibited George Wallace from seeking another term. However, the governor ran a shadow campaign, helping elect his wife, Lurleen, to office, which simultaneously gave him access to the travel and other resources of the office while allowing him freedom to plan a run for the White House in 1968.[320] As racial uprisings escalated in Watts, Detroit, and tensions flared in Milwaukee, Wallace blamed the lawlessness on the federal government for setting a bad example by defying the Constitution. He even went so far to argue that the federal government was in cahoots with Fidel Castro in "launching guerilla warfare in American cities."[321]

Peak of Milwaukee Civil Rights Activism

In the years after Wallace's initial campaign, the civil rights movement in Milwaukee reached its high-water mark. The failure of Milwaukee Public Schools (MPS) to address the MUSIC's goal of integration led to the group's coordinated boycott of the schools and the establishment of "freedom schools," where eleven thousand students learned African

American history and the concepts of freedom, brotherhood, justice and equality.[322] By July 1965, the NAACP had filed a lawsuit calling for the full integration of the MPS. The school board argued that this would not be possible due to the city's segregated housing.[323] While the group did not achieve its goal of desegregation, there were minor concessions from MPS, including increased hiring of Black teachers and an open enrollment program. The group also raised awareness of inequity in the community and demonstrated that sustained mass protest was achievable in Milwaukee.[324] Still, following the Bloody Sunday violence in Selma, Milwaukee was identified by the NAACP as a "do-nothing city" that had done little to eliminate de facto segregation.[325] Wallace's campaign had laid bare that there was strong opposition to civil rights in white communities in Milwaukee.[326]

The stage was set for a dramatic showdown between activists and the Wallace-supporting white neighborhoods in Milwaukee. The leader of the Black activists was an unlikely figure: a white priest, Father James Groppi, who returned from the Edmund Pettus Bridge with a sense of purpose to bring about social justice to his hometown.[327] Groppi first dove into the MUSIC campaign before shifting focus to open housing, an advocate of a militant nonviolent direct action. He believed it was through coercive nonviolence that society would be forced to face racial inequality and be transformed.[328] Building off priests' and nuns' roles in protesting Wallace's campaign, Groppi believed that his faith necessitated involvement in opposing racial injustice. By 1965, Groppi was advisor of Milwaukee's NAACP Youth Council, transforming the group into a force for militant action, establishing a Freedom House in the heart of the city.[329] When Milwaukee's NACCP's offices were bombed by a Wisconsin Klansman who worked for the Wallace campaign, the Youth Council armed themselves and stood guard in front of the Freedom House.[330]

In August 1966, Groppi led 150 members of the NAACP Youth Council from the city to suburban Wauwatosa to protest Judge Robert Cannon's membership to the Milwaukee Eagles Club, which barred Black people from joining. Angry white residents met the group, wielding signs drenched with obscenities, the n-word and promises to "Keep Tosa White."[331] On August 28, as the group crossed city limits, police had to separate white residents and the protesters as violence and tempers appeared to flare. The protests were the first time the Wisconsin National Guard was called out for a civil rights demonstration.[332] Despite the activists' efforts, there were no meaningful changes to the club's policies.[333]

The violence with which Groppi and the YC were met led to the creation of the Commandos, a group designed to defend nonviolent protesters with "not-violent" tactics, meaning that while they were unarmed (unlike the Black Panthers) and did not seek out a fight (like the Black Panthers), they were willing to defend themselves and fight back if needed, which according to Groppi was a "necessary survival method."[334] The group embraced a Black Power ideology blended with Christian theology, but many in the Black community worried the militant group might spark violence.[335]

By 1967, relations between the Black community and police had deteriorated, sparking unrest for three days in July. Fires and gunfire prompted Mayor Maier to call out the National Guard. In what became known as the 1967 Riot, 3 died, 100 were injured and 1,740 were arrested.[336] While not as deadly and destructive as the concurrent uprisings in Newark and Detroit, it demonstrated to many the plight and suffering in the Inner Core, while to others it confirmed the destabilizing effect of Black activists and necessitated law and order to regain control.[337]

On August 29, 1967, the confrontation between the YC and white Milwaukeeans reached its climax. Groppi led two hundred protesters across the Sixteenth Street Viaduct, which divided the predominantly Black north side with the south side, dominated by white working-class residents. Blocks from Serb Hall, where Wallace had fired up the crowd three years earlier, the viaduct was jokingly referred to as "the longest bridge in the world since it connected Africa to Poland."[338] As the protesters crossed the bridge, they were confronted by a crowd of hundreds of white residents who shouted, waved racist signs and wore Wallace stickers. The white mob abruptly rushed the marchers, overwhelming the police, and chaos ensued. Riot police were able to disperse the white crowd, and Groppi, refusing to retreat, continued his march to Kosciuszko Park. When the civil rights protesters returned to the city, their opponents assaulted them and burned down their Freedom House.[339]

The marchers pushed for open housing, which Alderwoman Vel Phillips had been pursuing futilely on the city council since 1962.[340] Undeterred, the group continued marches for fair housing for two hundred consecutive nights, and they gained national notoriety in the process. By September, more than five thousand marchers were crossing the viaduct to meet jeering crowds.[341] As Wisconsin winter set in, the protest evolved into a boycott of Milwaukee breweries and a "Black Christmas" (a call for Black residents to patronize only Black-owned businesses) to put pressure on businesses to support open housing.[342] While the mayor and council still continued to reject open housing, the death of Martin Luther King put federal emphasis on passage of a Fair Housing Act. Senator Walter Mondale discussed Milwaukee's housing marches on the Senate floor, and after the bill passed in 1968, the common council finally relented and passed "a citywide ordinance that surpassed the federal law."[343]

If Groppi united support among Black activists, his groups' efforts also galvanized white resistance. White counterdemonstrators were openly hostile to civil rights advocates, flaunting White Power signs, Wallace stickers and Confederate flags hundreds of miles north of Dixie.[344] Groups such as the White Power Rangers formed, garnering support from the Wallace supporters in the John Birch Society and National States' Rights Party.[345] Uniting ethnic divisions, thousands of white Milwaukeeans, believing their working-class communities under assault, held rallies attacking Groppi, chanting and wielding racist placards.[346] The stage was set for another clash, with the 1968 election as the backdrop.

THE CAMPAIGN BEGINS

Wallace returned to Wisconsin months before he even launched his official 1968 campaign. On June 16, 1967, Wallace landed in Milwaukee to a greeting of seventy-five supporters wearing "Wallace for President" pins and gifting him bouquets of carnations. In the terminal with a backdrop of signs that read "Stand up for America" and "Help Restore Sanity in Our Government," Wallace attacked the press, blasted opponents of the Vietnam War and denied accusations of bigotry and racism that he claimed hurt his chances in the state in 1964. He believed that as awareness grew about his real beliefs and positions, he would fare better in states like Wisconsin and hinted at his independent candidacy. In his typical federalism framework, Wallace argued that schools should determine their own integration policies without federal intervention, leaving room for schools to allow integration if it had local support.[347] A packed crowd at a hotel ballroom cheered wildly when Wallace promised to "take his movement 'the length and breadth of the land' to give people a choice in 1968."[348]

Despite flirting with entering the Democratic primaries in places like Wisconsin, Wallace decided to run as an independent candidate, taking on both Democrats and Republicans in the general election. This required a Herculean hurdle for the candidate: get enough signatures to get on the ballot in all fifty states.[349] With his wife battling and eventually succumbing to cancer, Wallace fought to secure his place on California's ballot and several other key states, cementing his American Independent Party candidacy. With Johnson's decision to not seek a second term due in large part to the tumultuous Vietnam War, Democrats nominated Hubert Humphrey, while the Republican nominee, Richard Nixon, hoped to court southern votes and saw the Alabamian as a threat to his electoral strategy.[350]

While Wallace flirted with scenarios in which he garnered enough southern support to win a plurality of the Electoral College, he did not realistically hope to win the presidency outright.[351] Rather, he hoped to get his name on as many ballots as possible and prevent the two major parties from winning the Electoral College. This would enable the governor to "extract big policy concessions on race in exchange for conceding the office."[352] He planned to then release his electoral votes to whichever candidate would make "a solemn covenant with the American people [to form]…a coalition government like they have in some other countries."[353] Wallace believed he would win enough southern states and only surrender those votes in exchange for passage of legislation he supported. By "spoiling" the election for either party, Wallace hoped to show that both parties had "spoiled the chances for the people."[354]

Wallace's party platform blamed the national government for doing nothing to correct the problems plaguing the United States, namely, chaos in cities, local control of schools and communities stripped of their authority, rising taxes and out-of-control welfare.[355] While he did not overtly argue the merits of the Tenth Amendment and states' rights over the Fourteenth Amendment, he lambasted the federal government as socialistic and evil. He blamed the Civil Rights Act for encouraging riots and lawlessness and promised to restore law and order and local control.[356]

When he all but declared his candidacy on *Meet the Press*, he downplayed overt racism, dog whistling with rhetoric of "law and order," while continuing to rail against big government.[357] Wallace said, "I don't talk about race or segregation anymore…we're talking about law and order and local control of schools, things like that." Nixon avoided trying to "out-Wallace Wallace," conceding states in the Deep South that Wallace would win and instead focusing on the southern states on the Atlantic Seaboard that would help him clinch the Electoral College. While Wallace was attracting huge crowds in northern cities, these were unlikely to translate into electoral victories.[358]

Wallace spoke vaguely about the Vietnam War, addressing only broad terms about patriotism and supporting troops, but tied his justification for clamping down on antiwar demonstrations to his law-and-order rhetoric. He fired up his blue-collar crowds by railing against "pseudo-intellectuals, Communists, anarchists and bureaucrats."[359]

Running a national campaign from August until November meant that Wallace could not focus as much on individual states like Wisconsin as he would have in a primary election. He did tours of the West, Midwest and Northeast, stopping in states for hours instead of weeks that a candidate could dedicate in a primary election. Wallace believed he could do well in Wisconsin, but his most likely path to success meant winning southern states, where he spent a large amount of his relatively finite resources as an independent candidate. Still, Wallace made two stops in the Badger State, both marked by dramatic confrontation with his supporters, who supported his Tenth Amendment arguments, and opponents, who attempted to disrupt and defeat the candidate in defense of equal protection rights.

A SHOWDOWN IN MILWAUKEE

On April 3, Wallace announced Lloyd Herbstreith as the head of his campaign in Wisconsin. He and his wife, Delores, had been instrumental in getting Wallace on the primary ballot four years earlier and began the process of collecting signatures to get him on the general election ballot as an independent in November.[360] The campaign made no effort to enter the Democratic primary in the spring, and Wallace made no campaign visits to the Badger state in the spring or summer.[361] Despite some filing issues (Wallace had put a placeholder vice presidential candidate on his nomination petitions before officially picking General Curtis LeMay as his running mate, which the state's secretary of state would not allow), Herbstreith was successful at getting Wallace on the ballot and twelve Wallace electors assigned.[362] When plans were finally set for a brief campaign stop in Milwaukee on September 12, supporters and opponents rallied their bases.

The clash between Wallace's supporters and opponents unfolded in three settings: the Sheraton-Schroeder Hotel and inside and outside the Milwaukee Auditorium. When Wallace touched down at Mitchell International Airport, supporters greeted him wearing Wallace buttons, and fifteen NAACP Youth Commandos shouted, "Here comes the pig!"[363] Lawrence Friend, Youth Council president, tried vainly to set up a meeting with Wallace to discuss integration. The Commandos tried to follow Wallace's motorcade procession to his first stop, a fundraising dinner at the Sheraton-Schroeder

Hotel. Wallace addressed a warm group of supporters, which he fired up by stating, "I expect to win."[364] Outside, sixty-five demonstrators from the NAACP Youth Council and the antiwar Youth Against War and Fascism confronted Wallace, picketing with signs stating, "Go Home Wallace: We Have Enough Racists," "Stop the War Against Blacks" and "US Racism Kills Here and in Vietnam."[365] The *Janesville Daily-Gazette* reported that one "unkempt" protester called a Wallace supporter a fascist bitch as the two groups ascended to the Auditorium.[366]

The rise of the civil rights movement in Wisconsin coincided with the emergence of Wallace as a national force. NAACP Youth Council Commandos united to try to disrupt Wallace's Wisconsin campaign. *Wisconsin Historical Society, WHI-(X3)37639.*

More than six thousand critics and supporters of Wallace converged on the Auditorium in Milwaukee to make their views of the Alabamian known. The *Milwaukee Journal* assessed the scene: "Following the 1968 fashion of politics by confrontation, two wings of the anti-establishment establishment stood eyeball to eyeball…and yelled at each other."[367] Around seven hundred were protesters, a large contingent from the NAACP Youth Council, with Father Groppi partaking in the march and protest. From when they first entered the facility at 7:30 p.m. to their planned coordinated departure at 9:00, the protesters disrupted the event by stomping in unison, chanting and holding up provocative signs.[368] Upon entering the room, protesters flashed V for victory signs and clashed with the predominantly pro-Wallace crowd. Covered disapprovingly by several papers, the protesters allegedly booed when the rally opened during the National Anthem and the Lord's Prayer.[369] A Wallace supporter viewed these actions with "disgust," wondering "what influence seems to be controlling the minds" of the protesters.[370]

Altercations broke out throughout the event. When one white supporter shouted, "Go home where you belong, n———!" one protester shot back, "This is youth here, not old folks!" Another paper described an altercation between a "burly negro" who shouted in a Wallace supporter's face,

Father Groppi and the Commandos were loud and tried to disrupt Wallace's Milwaukee rally, both inside and outside the auditorium. © Milwaukee Journal-Sentinel—*USA TODAY Network*.

"Bigots, who needs 'em?" to which the Wallace supporter responded, "You're a lousy communist."[371] A sixteen-year-old boy sat with opponents of Wallace, encouraging them to let him talk. "Let's give him the rights he denies others; Let's show him we're bigger than he is," the young man vainly implored.[372] A Racine woman lamented, "The principles of our forefathers are going down the drain [and] we can't let this continue."[373] A Wallace opponent egged on a supporter to punch him, and the supporter warned him not to push him too far.

The protesters held up signs that said, "If You Liked Hitler, You'll Love Wallace," and "Justice, Yes, Wallace, No!" Their chants ranged from threats to civil rights slogans, including "Kill Wallace," "Soul Power" and "Sieg Heil."[374] Wallace supporters far outnumbered the protesters, drowning out the jeers with "We Want Wallace!"[375]

When Wallace took the stage behind his traveling bulletproof podium, civil rights activists stood and constantly disrupted his speech by shouting, clapping, banging on cowbells and stomping.[376] A Wallace supporter from Stevens Point would later recall that "Groppi and his boys" created a "tremendous racket."[377] Wallace fired back several times, accusing the protesters of being Nazis, and charging, "The biggest bigots in the world are those who call others bigots."[378] To an enthusiastic crowd, Wallace railed against "anarchy in government" and pledged his support of police. As the protesters repeatedly interrupted, Wallace retorted, "I used to talk about anarchy. I don't have to. You can see it now," a reference to the law and order platform that he carved out as a response to what white supporters saw as the lawlessness of urban unrest.[379] Later, Wallace asked his supporters to "let the police" take care of the protesters, claiming they were just trying to get on television.[380] After about fifteen minutes, Groppi led the young activists in unison out of the Auditorium and into the street, where the protests continued.[381] As they left, Wallace retorted, "These are the folks that people are sick and tired of in this country," going on to add that they better have their say now because "after November 5th, you're through. You're through!"[382] Joking minutes later, Wallace said, "They're outside now, maybe crossing the street. I hope they get hit by a car."[383]

Papers reported that the blue-collar white supporters were now alone to rain cheer and praise on the governor. Many wore Wallace stickers on their clothes and foreheads, and many eagerly dropped donations into buckets scattered throughout the room.[384] The *Waukesha Daily Freeman* described a revival-like atmosphere and claimed that the governor "socked it to 'em."[385] Wallace's event began with theatrics to get the crowd riled up: a country

NAACP Youth Council members jeer and taunt Wallace during a raucous rally in Milwaukee. *From the* Capital Times, *reprinted with permission.*

music performance and a "well-endowed" cowgirl in a skintight Wallace suit.[386] The crowd needed no extra motivation, however, as the governor's speech brought them to frenzy. Wallace criticized high federal taxes and pledged to restore local control to his supporters' communities in Wisconsin. "We are going to turn back to the people of this state the absolute control of schools," Wallace crooned. "Not one dime of federal tax money is going to be spent to require you bus your child to anywhere in Milwaukee."[387] Picking up on his federalism theme four years earlier, Wallace promised "return back to the people of this state [local] control."[388] He praised Milwaukee police for making it "safe to walk the streets." While not going too deeply into his foreign policy, he pledged to end the Vietnam War. The largest and most sustained applause came when he blasted the federal open housing law, claiming that both Nixon and Humphrey supported the legislation.[389]

Thanking the crowd for "getting the movement started" four years earlier, Wallace blasted intellectuals, authors of the Kerner Report and media critics, saying "Let the *Milwaukee Journal* read it and weep."[390]

Around fifteen Youth Commandos attempted to force their way into the Auditorium after the doors were closed, leading to an additional couple of thousand supporters and opponents gathering outside the facility on Kilbourn Avenue during the speech. One of the Commandos shouted, "Hey, we've got a right to be in there," while others pounded on the glass doors. After failing to enter, the Commandos pushed their way through the crowd and organized a protest, chanting, "Black Power!"[391] Following the rally, the protesters burned Wallace pennants, and Groppi and other leaders led a march around the Auditorium before heading to the Youth Council

White supporters of Wallace packed the Auditorium in Milwaukee, drowning out the protests with thunderous applause. *Photo by Archie Lieberman, reprinted with permission.*

headquarters, "trading taunts" with Wallace supporters.[392] Despite the willingness of the Commandos to use violence in self-defense, and despite the violent clashes months earlier when leaders crossed the viaduct, there was no violence between the groups and only three were arrested.[393] It had been a tense, spirited and boisterous battle, but a peaceful one.

A FOOD FIGHT IN OSHKOSH

Wallace continued his national campaign, zigzagging the nation and drawing passionate crowds. According to his campaign manager Bill Jones, however, he made a tactical error by focusing time and effort on the West Coast and Mountain West, where his support was small and tepid, rather than on areas where he had strong support.[394] Still, it appeared Wallace was poised to do well in the South and could compete to take second in five other states.[395] On October 17, the Wallace campaign announced two more stops in the Badger State the following week in Oshkosh and Racine during his final trip through the Midwest before the general election.[396] On October 22, Wallace arrived in the Fox Valley, and much of the drama of rhetoric and reaction resumed. The crowds in Oshkosh and Racine were again a mix of supportive and hostile, and like in 1964, the opposition was largely allies of Black civil rights activists, since there were not large populations of African Americans in these places.

Students at the University of Wisconsin–Oshkosh (then Oshkosh State) clashed over the Wallace visit. Members of the conservative Young Americans for Freedom (YAF) chapter planned a welcome reception with signs and invited protesters, who, according to one of the local chapter's leaders, Wallace was superb at handling. Young Democrats and Students for a Democratic Society also prepared for the visit, passing out leaflets encouraging students to bring balloons to pop to disrupt the speech.[397]

A small crowd of one hundred people met Wallace when he landed at Winnebago County Airport, including Lloyd and Delores Herbstreith, the twelve electors who would cast their votes if the third party candidate won and the Oshkosh YAF chairman.[398] He had spent the night before in Milwaukee and taken a charter plane to the Fox Valley the next morning.[399] While the crowd was apparently disappointing to the campaign, there were also no anti-Wallace demonstrators there.[400] After a photo session, Wallace's motorcade took him to Monument Square in downtown Oshkosh. There a crowd of more than eight thousand greeted and jeered

Wallace faced a hostile crowd on his second and final campaign stop in Oshkosh.
© Appleton Post Crescent—*USA TODAY Network.*

Wallace's brief twenty-five-minute speech on the cold, windy and rainy fall Wisconsin day.[401]

Beneath a memorial for Union soldiers, the southerner again credited his 1964 Wisconsin primary as the beginning of his presidential bid and predicted he would carry the state's twelve electoral votes.[402] As several papers noted, Wallace's speech lacked new proposals but highlighted some of his regular campaign arguments. He again rejected federal intrusion into issues that he believed should be left to local control. Wallace promised to end the Vietnam War if elected but did not comment on his running mate's fact-finding trip to Indochina that had just concluded. Promising to both "bring the boys home" and restore America's military, he also reiterated his "law and order" stance, accusing Democrats and Republicans of both being soft on crime and failing at the federal level.[403] Despite denying racism and stating that he hoped to have support of all races, Wallace spent the bulk of his speech railing on racial issues, including federal efforts in education, union seniority and housing. Interestingly, a repeal of federal housing laws would have been moot in Oshkosh, since they had locally passed stronger fair housing legislation, apparently unbeknownst to Wallace.[404]

Throughout the speech, hecklers and protesters, including a large contingent of students from Oshkosh State, regularly interrupted Wallace. Prior to the downtown speech, students held a protest rally on campus, wielding signs that stated, "Wallace is America's Psychosomatic Disorder" and "Stand up for Bigotry."[405] As students descended downtown, some marched in with Nazi flags and banners, with signs that said, "Wallace is America's Hillbilly Hitler," "Sieg Heil, Y'all" and one that had a photo of Wallace with a Hitler mustache.[406] Students popped and squeakily rubbed balloons loudly throughout the speech, booing and chanting, "Go home!"[407] Though less provocative, Wallace supporters' signs vastly outnumbered the protesters, including ones that read, "Let George Do it in '68," "Wallace for President" and "Welcome Mr. President."[408] One reporter noted a working-class woman in a weathered fur coat mumbling under her breath as Wallace spoke, "He's right…he's right, I don't care what my son says, he's right…"[409] Two Waukesha teens would recall their experience meeting Wallace during his visit. Lana Luddington described Wallace as "sweet and kind," and appreciated his willingness to talk to the people. Cheryl Yuker said she supported Wallace because he stood for "law and order" and "he's not a racist, even though people say he is."[410] Another Wisconsinite backed Wallace because she supported his stance on "racial problems," adding, "He has good policies to settle disorders in the United States."[411]

As always, Wallace took pleasure in stirring up his supporters by attacking the protesters, branding them anarchists and warning a hippie he had boll weevils in his beard. After being barraged by obscenities, he suggested two four-letter words with which he said protesters were unfamiliar: "W-O-R-K" and "S-O-A-P."[412] He called out to a male protester with long hair, "Hi sweetie! Oh I thought you were a she!"[413] After multiple eggs and food scraps from the crowd missed their mark, an apple core was thrown onto the platform, hitting the backdrop and splattering on Wallace's overcoat from behind his bulletproof podium, causing him to flinch.[414] Wallace shrugged off the work of an "anarchist" and continued his speech, which he was able to complete with the help of his powerful microphones over the loud and frequent protests.[415] However, a reporter traveling with Wallace said that Oshkosh had been the largest contingent of hecklers he had seen on the campaign trail.[416] Wallace claimed to reporters that the protesters only helped him, since they represented "what this country is tired of."[417]

In the middle of his speech in Oshkosh, Wallace was struck by an apple core. © Milwaukee Journal—*USA TODAY Network.*

Following his short speech in Oshkosh, a plane whisked Wallace away to Milwaukee, where he traveled by motorcade to Racine for a 5:00 p.m. rally at Memorial Hall followed by a fundraising dinner at the Racine Motor Inn. Prior to his arrival, the head of the Racine branch of the NAACP, Julian Thomas, announced that their local executive board had voted to ignore the local rally. In a departure from the Milwaukee NAACP's tactics in September, Thomas said that the NAACP believed in freedom of speech and the group would allow Wallace to speak without interference. This move earned the NAACP commendation from Racine's mayor, William Beyer, who lauded the group for "showing their fine sense of responsibility as citizens."[418]

Memorial Hall was packed with about 3,500 people, again both supporters and opponents of Wallace.[419] Wallace repeated many topics covered in Oshkosh, including his pledge to restore safety to America's failing cities. Despite the NAACP boycott, about 400 to 600 protesters were there, waving placards calling for a silent protest. Eventually, these protesters walked out and were replaced by Wallace supporters waiting outside.[420] Other protesters were not so serene, including one "leather-lunged" protester who repeatedly challenged Wallace's antiunion right-to-work policies.[421] Another protester challenged the governor to talk about Selma, a reference to the voting rights protests three years earlier. Wallace invited the heckler to come down and see it "and jump off the bridge if you want to."[422] After talking about the strong African American support Lurleen received in her run for governor,

Wallace fired up his supporters by railing against open housing laws. He criticized Nixon for supporting a congressional committee to explore a one world government initiative, which he argued would further eviscerate local control by having police from Africa patrolling the streets of Racine.[423] Wallace also criticized federal gun controls, which he argued would strip law-abiding Wisconsinites of weapons while "every thug would have a machine gun."[424]

Wallace closed the evening by speaking to around three hundred supporters at a fundraising dinner, which had jovial country music and the campaign sharing high hopes of an Electoral College win.[425] He spent the night in Milwaukee before heading out on the final leg of his tour of the North, including an electric reception at Madison Square Garden in New York.[426] Despite the chaos, Wallace was pleased with the crowds and welcome he received.[427] Despite the raucous crowd and heavy police and secret service presence, there were no arrests in Oshkosh and only three in Racine for disorderly conduct when protesters pressed up against the governor's motorcade.[428] After his visit, anecdotal evidence and polling showed gains for Wallace. A survey by the *Beloit Daily News* found 35 percent of voters favored Wallace in the six-county area along the border with Illinois.[429] An Associated Press poll found Wallace trailing with only 14.5 percent but gaining ground in four of the state's communities.[430] The governor would not return to the Badger State again before the November election, but his brief, tumultuous visits cemented cultural and constitutional divisions that began four years earlier.

REACTION TO WALLACE'S CAMPAIGN AND VISITS

As any pundit could have predicted, Wallace's brief stops in Wisconsin drew stark and varied assessments from the press, elected leaders and the community at large. Despite only two visits, there was significant, passionate and divisive debate about the Wallace candidacy throughout Wisconsin in the fall of 1968.

Many letters to the editor showed support or at least sympathy for Wallace in the wake of his campaign stops. One letter to the *Milwaukee Journal* blasted the paper for defaming Wallace and accused it of promoting "race mixing" and attempting to "destroy the Nordic race" that the Lord created, which would lead to a "race suicide."[431] The *Fond du Lac Reporter* noted that Wallace had "attracted a wide following in Wisconsin."[432] One union member wrote to the *La Crosse Tribune* that he and other machinists were backing Wallace, not Humphrey, as their leaders were pushing. The author blasted Humphrey for being "for Negroes' rights," promoting urban unrest and denying "our right of free choice."[133] A piece in the *Fond du Lac Reporter* described Wallace's campaign as gaining increased acceptability from a wide array of votes and finding a "deep chord of response, a way of strumming hard on assorted discontents."[134]

A Sheboygan resident wrote a letter to the *Milwaukee Sentinel* imploring Wallace supporters to stick to their convictions and not cave in and vote for one of the other candidates for fear that Wallace "can't win anyway."[135] Another supporter argued that Wallace offered a true alternative to the "baloney" of the major parties, which offered no solutions to the problems the nation faced.[136] A Green Bay resident echoed this line of reasoning, blasting Nixon's and Humphrey's policies and praising Wallace for bringing conservative stances back into the mainstream.[137] Others believed in his common-sense solutions to difficult issues facing the country.[138] A Brookfield man praised Wallace for "having the courage to say what is on the people's minds" and standing with people who are "fed up with riots, demonstrations, immorality, dope, and all other manifestations of a degenerate society." He went on to reject that law and order was code for racism, saying it simply stood for restoring order to the streets.[139]

Others attacked the "ultra-liberal press" for not giving Wallace a fair shake. A resident wrote to the *Wausau Daily Herald*, blasting the paper for neglecting where Wallace stood on issues, going on a diatribe to "inform" readers about Wallace. Among the concerns were that "deadbeats" had more rights than "law-abiding citizens"; Washington bureaucrats had too much power in deciding who "you must rent to, sell to, or hire"; and that police should not have to "stand idle while people loot, riot and burn."[140] Another letter in the same issue blasted a business owner who fired an employee for wearing a Wallace pin.[141] Still others attacked a local paper for suggesting that Wallace was racist, when in fact he could prevent riots that Vel Phillips and other civil rights leaders were responsible for bringing to Milwaukee.[142]

While other papers did not support Wallace, several, including the *Racine Journal Times*, the *Marshfield News Herald* and the *Neenah News Record*, implored critics to stay home and "let him speak his piece," arguing that such disruptions to campaigns were a "national disgrace."[143]

Countering these supporters were a sizable number of Wallace critics and opponents. Following his rally in Milwaukee, Wallace's campaign office on

West Lincoln Avenue had windows damaged by a pellet gun.[444] An editorial in the *Milwaukee Sentinel* called on labor leaders to reject Wallace's "plain language campaign," which offered "no room for compromise" and led to his success four years earlier.[445] The *Racine-Journal Times* showed concern that Wallace's campaign was picking up momentum, and though it was unlikely he would win, he had potential to shift the election or throw it into electoral chaos. Tex Reynolds also expressed surprise that Wallace found support outside of the fringes of the electorate, paraphrasing Shakespeare: "Not that I think he's the perfect answer, but I love less what's going on in this country."[446]

A letter to the editor responded by blasting Wallace, wondering how the governor from a state with the highest murder rates could be the candidate of law and order and how Wallace could rail against federal spending when Alabama "takes $3 from the federal government for every $1 of state money."[447] An editorial published in the *Eau Claire Leader Telegram* criticized Wallace's choice of Curtis LeMay as his running mate, saying they were a perfect pair since Wallace was myopic on domestic affairs and LeMay was myopic on foreign affairs.[448] Another worried that the election of Wallace would lead to "one nation, under martial law," and criticized those who would ignore the racial undertones of his states' rights claims.[449]

A Milwaukee resident blasted the *Journal* for helping Wallace by covering his events, omitting details and not properly labeling him as racist.[450] Another letter said that Wallace was unequipped to bring the country together or resolve the "drift toward apartheid," warning that if Wallace was elected, "we can stop asking the silly question: How did Hitler happen?"[451] A West Bend resident warned readers of Wallace's association with the John Birch Society, which espoused hateful intolerance and denial of liberties defined in the Bill of Rights under a benign veil of religion and patriotism.[452] One letter joked that the parking meters in Racine, which were covered with red hoods during his visit, should have been white like a Klansman.[453] The *Wisconsin Jewish Chronicle* claimed Wallace and his supporters' demand for local control was a way of achieving "American apartheid, but on their own white terms."[454] A letter to the *Capital Times* warned that Wallace's support would serve as a barometer for how much racial intolerance and racism still existed in the state and nation, while another said Wallace supporters would "waste a vote on racism."[455] An op-ed piece in the *Wisconsin Rapids Daily Tribune* called Wallace a con man who preyed on Wisconsinites' fears and avoided directly invoking race but used law and order as a shield for his "raging bigotry."[456]

State AFL-CIO president John Schmitt mocked Wallace as an "anti-governor" who was an enemy of organized labor at a labor event in Oshkosh.[457] Republican Illinois senator Charles Percy spoke to a crowd of Republicans in Madison, stating that Wallace "represents the worst in American life" and was "more frightening than any of the specters he is raising on the campaign."[458] Milwaukee mayor Maier branded Wallace as a "'white supremacist militant' who was not qualified to be president and would harm Milwaukee and other large cities if elected."[459] Democratic senator Gaylord Nelson speculated that Wallace support would hurt the Democrat Humphrey more than the Republican Nixon in Wisconsin.[460]

BLACK WISCONSINITES RESPONSE TO WALLACE

In addition to participating in the demonstrations at Wallace's Milwaukee event, the Black community weighed in on the Wallace candidacy in the press and in speeches, although less intensely than they had in 1964. The *Milwaukee Courier* featured an opinion piece by Whitney M. Young Jr. that argued that despite the heavy focus and rhetoric on "law and order," there was little concrete discussion on how tangibly to improve police protection. Young speculated that this was likely because "law and order" was used by Wallace "as a code phrase for stopping racial demonstrations and in general keeping the Black man in his place."[461] Still sanguine, Young hoped that other non-bigoted candidates would use the phrase as a place to launch a Presidential Conference on Police and Justice to recommend meaningful steps to improve policing and police-community relations. He called for reform by citing examples of police brutality against Black Panthers, as well as the presence of Klansmen in the police ranks. Young suggested better pay to attract and reward good officers and better crowd control training for police responding to "a few black militants." Training, he maintained, should replace tanks and riot gear so that the Black community, "which suffers most from crime but gets the least protection" can see value in policing.[462]

Another editorial claimed that Wallace's appeal was primarily emotional, and that if enacted, his actual policies would "bring us to the brink of civil war."[463] He speculated that a civil war would be fine with Wallace supporters, since they had "the necessary strength on their side."[464] He noted that Wallace's strength outside the South lay in the lower middle class, since they have "felt the brunt of the black revolution and the revolt of the children of affluence."[465] Another editorial piece in the *Milwaukee Star* branded Wallace

Above: A cartoon in the *Milwaukee Star* examines Wallace's "law and order" rhetoric. *Provided by the* Milwaukee Courier.

Right: The *Milwaukee Courier* portrays Wallace as a racist monster and warns Black voters to vote. *Provided by the* Milwaukee Courier.

a "hate peddler" who used fear and his "cure all remedy of law and order" on his blind supporters. His remedy, however, did not provide the cure, but was "tainted by the most insidious of all poisons—'HATRED.'"[466]

The *Milwaukee Courier* and *Milwaukee Star* each employed political cartoons to ridicule Wallace and his bigoted policies. One had Wallace as the face of a monster, spreading his tentacles across the country. The monster, spewing the governor's "Segregation Forever" inaugural address, was labeled "George Wallace, Racist." The cartoonist warned voters that "they are asking for it" unless they register to vote.[467] Another cartoon satirized Wallace's "law and order" stance by portraying white policemen with fangs, beady eyes and pointy ears, handing out "Wallace for President" pins. As one of the white officers hands a pin to a distressed Black officer in the middle of the pack, he says, "Take a button and pass them down."[468]

Comedian and activist Dick Gregory spoke in Madison, encouraging supporters to back his third-party candidacy, despite state restrictions on write-in candidates. Pledging that he was the most honest, loyal and "statesman of the lot," Gregory called out Wallace and his law and order rhetoric. He argued law and order "is a hip way of saying n———" and that his opponents' call for toughness on crime was only targeted at the "poor and uneducated, not the wealthy big-time criminals." Blasting capitalists for disregarding constitutional principles, Gregory said, "Damn the Constitution, 'cause it's not enforced today," closing his address with a clenched fist signifying Black Power.[469]

Leading up to the race, The *Milwaukee Star* used Wallace as motivation to exercise the vote that many "black men died for."[470] Asking readers how they would feel if they were watching television at home and election results "declare George Wallace as the next president of the United States? It could happen! But ONLY IF you fail to exercise your American privilege and vote."[471] The paper warned that while young Black leaders were picketing and fighting for equality,

> *We have a candidate who stands before racist audiences in the HEART OF THE NORTH, and bigoted audiences all over the United States. These racists are going to vote AGAINST…equality. They are already multiplying their forces and surging to the polls to REGISTER so they can continue to keep the black man in his place.*[472]

Wallace was certainly less of a focus for the Black press in 1968 than he was four years earlier. The disjointed campaign without a short and targeted primary as well as the growth of the civil rights movement in Milwaukee made Wallace an important, but not central foil to their goals and did not merit their full attention.

PASSIONATE SUPPORT, BUT POOR SHOWING

Wallace was able to attract raucous crowds outside of Dixie, including an American Legion post in Wisconsin, finding every chance he could to appeal to white voters' resentment.[473] Though he had limits to his advertising, he drew large crowds, including six thousand in Milwaukee and a raucous crowd at Madison Square Garden in New York City.[474] Wallace's rhetoric continued to instill fear of an overarching federal government "stomping all over states' rights."[475] It was blue-collar workers who were ignored by bureaucrats. Key to Wallace's support was his base of support among bigoted Klansmen and John Birchers, but while courting their support, the governor was careful to note that he himself did not belong to these organizations. He claimed publicly that he planned and campaigned to win, and when he did, he intended to pass laws limiting federal authority and appoint conservative justices to the Supreme Court.[476]

Wallace had high hopes for a strong showing in Wisconsin. He tried to capitalize on the racial tensions in Milwaukee and campus unrest in Madison, believing that both would lead to a groundswell of support for a message of "law and order." While calling for a crackdown, he somewhat contradictorily called for less involvement by the federal government. The message was intended for white, working-class constituents.[477] The choice of Curtis LeMay (who seemed willing to use nuclear weapons in Vietnam and made disastrous off-the-cuff responses on the campaign trail), however, as his vice presidential candidate, as well as Nixon's campaign warning that a "divided vote" would help Humphrey, hurt Wallace's support. Humphrey also climbed in the polls in many northern states, dooming Wallace's hopes north of the Mason-Dixon line.[478]

On Election Day, Wallace performed well by the standards of a third-party candidate but fell well short of the presidency. Winning several states in the heart of the former Confederacy, Wallace captured forty-six electoral votes and nearly 13 percent of the popular vote nationally. In the end, however, he was a distant third behind Humphrey and the president-elect, Richard Nixon.

Wallace ultimately underperformed in Wisconsin, winning only 7.6 percent of the vote, capturing less than 10 percent of the working-class vote in Milwaukee and failing to crack double digits in conservative rural towns.[479] In the Fox Valley, an area of strength four years earlier and a campaign stop, Wallace mustered only 7 percent of the vote.[480] While he faltered in the Badger State, he likely tipped the state and several others to Republican Nixon, perhaps delivering Nixon the presidency.[481] While these numbers were disappointing for Wallace, and seemingly lower than his campaign four years ago, it is worth noting that this was a general election, not a primary race. In spite of strong partisanship and structural and logistical disadvantages that plague independent campaigns, Wallace still managed to muster higher numbers than most third-party candidates.

Wallace and Wisconsin's civil rights movement hit their peaks simultaneously in and around the 1968 presidential campaign. Their direct encounters were brief, but the clashes were passionate and lively, as both tried to bring attention to their constitutional arguments through words and action. While both gained a national spotlight and notoriety, in many ways both fell short of their political objectives. And while this would not be the last time that their paths crossed, the height of the prominence and power of both would wane in some significant ways.

1972 PRESIDENTIAL CAMPAIGN, THE BEGINNING OF THE END

THE DECLINE OF DIRECT ACTION IN MILWAUKEE

Following the 1968 presidential election, serious schisms developed in the civil rights movement in Milwaukee. A year earlier, the Commandos had splintered into two groups, one more willing to work for institutional reform, while the other wanted to continue to push back from outside the system. By November 1968, Groppi had resigned as advisor to the YC.[482]

Despite the collapse of the YC as a formidable force, direct action continued, including a protest against company Allen Bradley for discrimination in hiring practices. Groppi and protesters pledged to picket the company until it hired more minorities. Again bringing national attention to the city, protesters were able to get some limited commitments from the company.[483]

In 1969, an alliance of Hispanic and Black civil rights leaders organized the Welfare Mothers March on Madison to put pressure on the Wisconsin State Assembly to resume welfare payments that were cut from the state budget.[484] Phillips and Groppi were among the organizers, but it was predominantly women marching from Milwaukee until joining forces with students and other groups in Madison. The crowd pushed into the state assembly chamber, until the governor called the National Guard to regain control of the Capitol. Groppi and a half-dozen others were arrested.[485] In 1971, the Milwaukee Black Panther Party emerged as a group supporting "armed self-defense."[486] While the group failed to break through in a significant way, it provided social services to inner core residents in the early 1970s.[487]

By the time Wallace's 1972 campaign was underway, direct action in Milwaukee had all but ended and was replaced by "an era of community organizing and cultural and electoral politics."[488] The civil rights groups had fought along specified policy initiatives, finding mixed success.

TIMES ARE A CHANGIN' FOR WALLACE

In 1971, a change in Alabama law allowed George Wallace to run and win another term as governor. He had remarried; his new wife, Cornelia, was a former beauty queen, singer and actress. Despite the success, Wallace was eyeing another run for president, believing that he had a shot at the Democratic nomination. He claimed to moderate his positions, arguing that segregation was no longer a desirable policy, while privately he appeared to retain his prejudicial views.[489] As his candidacy was forming, federal courts issued rulings supporting busing as a remedy to de facto segregation. Wallace was able to latch onto the white backlash against federal authority among white communities across the United States, especially in the North, which were vehemently opposed to sending their children to schools they perceived to be inferior and uncomfortable with Black children attending their community schools.[490]

When questioned by the *Washington Post* who he planned to have as policy advisors, Wallace blasted federal bureaucrats and experts for creating five decades of war and crippling debt, evoking a states' rights populism that was a through line in his campaigns.[491] Wallace used the busing issue to his advantage.[492] He argued that his opposition to busing was not racist; it was rather simply in opposition to "the idea that the federal government was impinging on what should be people's basic rights."[493] While arguing that community schools should exercise "freedom of choice," the disparate impact of such a stance would mean that schools would remain segregated and unequal. Wallace regularly argued that the oppressive federal government encroached on the average man's "home—his community—his domestic institutions, including his schools and in his associations with his fellow man."[494]

Despite the declining role of direct action and Wallace's truncated Wisconsin run, constitutional divisions between Wallace supporters and the state's Black community were still visible and the dialogue between federalism and equal protection continued.

Country Music, Muted Crowds in Milwaukee

After winning the Florida primary convincingly, Wallace decided to "test his strength in the North" by entering the Wisconsin primary. He entered the race on February 24 but was hesitant to campaign aggressively because he thought it would be embarrassing to his campaign if he were soundly defeated. His polling showed only 8 percent support in the Badger State, roughly equivalent to his showing in 1968. Although the numbers were disappointing, he changed his mind and began a whirlwind campaign effort on March 23, only eight days before the election.[195]

Despite having momentum, Wallace faced a crowded field in Wisconsin. Thirteen candidates were on the ballot in the Democratic primary. Hubert Humphrey, George McGovern, Edward Muskie, Henry Jackson, Eugene McCarthy, John Lindsay and Shirley Chisholm were among those crisscrossing the state, vying for crowds and media attention. According to pollster Patrick Caddell, to increase Wallace's support in Wisconsin from where they predicted, around 8 percent, to its highest potential, up to 30 percent, the campaign focused less on ideological and racial issues and more on tax reform and feelings of neglect among blue-collar workers.[496] Wallace used federal failures in Vietnam, claiming that southerners were "tired of the central government flim-flam."[497]

A buoyed Wallace crammed in eleven rallies and a barrage of TV interviews. While focusing on busing in Florida, Wallace pivoted to concerns of Wisconsinites, pledging he would "move for meaningful tax relief."[498] Upon arriving in Milwaukee, he blasted liberals in Washington for creating a "bottomless pit of taxation" that he predicted would result in a revolt. Wallace claimed that Wisconsinites' taxes were being wasted on foreign aid and "welfare loafers."[499] Wallace rejected involuntary busing as an assault on local control of schools, but he acknowledged (belatedly) that integration of public schools was "the law."[500] He attacked his competitors, most of whom he pointed out were senators whose failed federal policies in Vietnam, spending and taxation had created the mess voters found themselves in.[501]

Wallace's first rally on March 23 was back at the scene of the raucous event four years earlier, the Milwaukee Auditorium. While the 1968 scene was electric as a result of shouting matches and tense conflicts between Youth Commandos and Wallace backers, the scene four years later was different. It had the feel of an "open party," as Nashville country artists got the crowd fired up and young women passed around collection buckets before Wallace took the stage.[502] The *Milwaukee Journal* described it as a "fascinating show" that

Wallace speaks at a rally to kick off his 1972 campaign. *From the* Capital Times, *reprinted with permission.*

deep down was "serious business." After a local Medal of Honor recipient led the crowd of 4,600 in the Pledge of Allegiance, Wallace took the stage, to his supporters' delight.[503] His pivot to tax policy became apparent immediately, as Wallace jeered, "The average man who pays taxes and works each day for a living and holds this country together gets ignored, except on election day and on taxpaying day."[504] The reference to taxation got the loudest roars of support throughout the night. Wallace railed against the establishment in Washington and the Democratic Party for ignoring the plight of the working (white) man. Bashing the "six senators" he was running against, he claimed that in their 109 combined years of experience in Washington, they had done nothing to provide tax relief. Wallace promised that a win for Wallace in Wisconsin would mean "something will be done about tax reform even before the election!"[505]

Wallace also addressed inflation, which he blamed on federal spending and an expansive bureaucracy. Wallace discussed his trips to Washington, where he saw federal building after building and met "the assistant to the assistant to the assistant…making $25,000 to $40,000" carrying around briefcases filled with only a peanut butter sandwich.[506] While Wallace considered welfare for the "elderly, the blind, the halt and the maimed" appropriate, he attacked "welfare loafers and chiselers."[507] Wallace promised more responsible and limited government if he was elected president.

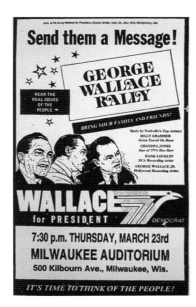

Wallace held his rallies with a country band to fire up the crowd, but spectators were more muted in 1972 than they had been in previous campaigns. *From the* Wisconsin State Journal, *reprinted with permission.*

Wallace was amused that his "law and order" rhetoric had become more mainstream but wondered why nobody in Washington had done anything to make Wisconsin safer. While he anticipated attacks as being an evil and out-of-touch candidate, Wallace warned the crowd, "They are not trying to get rid of George Wallace, they are trying to get rid of you."[508] In regards to busing, it was clear that Wallace intended to pivot away from the issue, referring to it as only a "philosophical" issue in Wisconsin.[509]

The *Milwaukee Journal* reported that the event was smaller and the crowd was less enthusiastic than four years earlier, with empty seats and many people in the crowd not cheering, but watching out of curiosity.[510] The verbal spats between civil rights groups and Wallace supporters that energized the room were gone with the era of direct action.

Outside the Auditorium, approximately 375 picketers gathered, and a handful made their way into the Auditorium. One carried a sign that read, "Hitler Lives in Alabama."[511] Like the audience inside, however, the protesters were also more subdued than four years earlier. After meeting at 6:00 p.m. at the civic center and listening to "antiwar and anti-administration harangues," members of a variety of groups, including Youth Against War and Fascism, the Committee to Free Angela Davis and students from UW-Milwaukee, marched to the Auditorium. Protesters marched and held signs that included "We Want Wallace…With a Rope Around His Neck!"[512] Almost all of the protesters decided to stay outside, and the protest ended as Wallace's speech began, meaning that unlike four years earlier, there would be no clash between picketers and Wallace supporters leaving the event.[513]

WALLACE'S REVIVAL TOUR
GETS ROARS AND THE SILENT TREATMENT

Avoiding a long stay in the liberal college town, where he was unlikely to garner support, Wallace "quietly" went to Madison to record a speech that would air the night before the election and take part in a television interview. Wallace said in the interview that he was unfairly painted as a racist by the media and that he "could make inroads into the Black vote if he had the chance to meet with Blacks."[514] Wallace went on to claim that minorities would fare better under his presidency than his opponents, since "I'm in touch with the problems that plague them," including high taxes, which he argued disproportionately affected people of color.[515] In the speech, Wallace called on Wisconsin voters to give Washington politicians a "jolt." By voting for him, Wallace argued, Wisconsinites could "send a message loud and clear to Washington that you want a change of direction."[516]

Wallace brought his revival tour next to Green Bay, getting a clamoring reception when he told the 1,400 people in attendance "taxes are too high."[517] The *Green Bay Press Gazette* noted that Wallace railed against welfare cheats, dope addicts, crime and foreign aid, but the crowd of mostly "middle class, somber faces" cheered the loudest when he claimed the federal government took too much of their hard-earned money.[518] The paper noted, however, that the "hour-long speech was almost devoid of any positive proposals" to remedy the many ills Wallace cited.[519] The only actual policy that the paper could find in the speech was a proposal by Wallace that rather than life appointments, the Supreme Court justices should be "acted upon" (by voters, the Congress or the president) every six to eight years.[520] This reform was consistent with Wallace's criticism of an activist federal court that wielded too much power over the states and the people and was certainly a response to the most recent decisions on busing that were unpopular in parts of the North. Denying at an earlier press conference that he was a demagogue, he pointed out that his competitors now adopted many of his ideas that branded him a "bad man" four years ago. Wallace claimed, "If every Wisconsinite could see me and hear me," they'd vote for him.[521]

On March 28, Wallace went to La Crosse and found a crowd receptive to the anti-tax message he was selling. The *Milwaukee Journal* noticed, adding, "Wallace is packing them in, be they curious or committed, and his campaign is apt to cause reverberations far louder than the electric guitars" at his rallies.[522] La Crosse had been on the losing side of a 1971 state shared tax redistribution formula, and his message of tax relief resonated with the

Wallace fires up a crowd of supporters at a campaign rally in La Crosse. *Photograph by Steven Noffke, provided by the* La Crosse Tribune.

crowd.[523] The crowd roared when Wallace said, "The average working man, farmer, and businessman is fed up to the gills of paying people not to work."[524] An overflow crowd of 4,500 packed Mary E. Sawyer Auditorium, with police estimating an additional 400 being turned away. Wallace railed against bureaucratic incompetence and stressed tax relief, pointing to Alabama's paltry property tax rates compared to Wisconsin.[525] "We don't believe in penalizing the taxpayer," Wallace claimed, although it was not clear if his figures included taxes for schools like Wisconsin.[526] Calling on voters to help him get their "message across" on taxation, he also blasted federal bureaucratic inefficiency, joking, "If you hire one bureaucrat, you have to hire two more to give him something to do, then four more to tell those two what to do, then eight more to tell those four what to do, and then sixteen to tell those eight what to do."[527] He again denounced welfare, claiming such programs would "break every city, county, state and taxpayer in the nation."[528] Clarifying his earlier stance, he called for a constitutional amendment that would require Congress to reconfirm or reject federal judges every six to eight years, claiming, "A federal judge has more power by the stroke of his pen than all the elected officials in the state of Wisconsin."[529]

After the speech ended, hundreds swarmed Wallace on stage to get autographs and flood praise at the candidate.

After a day trip to Tennessee, Wallace was back in Wisconsin the evening of the twenty-ninth in the middle of a snowstorm. Learning of Wallace's first campus stop at Lawrence University in Appleton, three hundred students, faculty and administrators planned and discussed several strategies to protest Wallace's speech, many believing his presence was inconsistent with university and student values. Tactics discussed included turning their backs to Wallace, inviting townspeople to a community-student discussion of Wallace's candidacy and obstructing the chapel's entrance.[530]

Ultimately, the protesters decided on the silent treatment. With polls showing Wallace in fourth place in the state primary, Wallace found a reception "as frigid as the wintry weather" at Lawrence University, with a majority of the crowd of 1,400 in the chapel remaining silent throughout his speech.[531] Wallace quipped, "I do appreciate your tumultuous welcome," but only a couple of hundred were moved to applause throughout his speech.[532]

Black students walk out in the middle of Wallace's speech at Lawrence University as many white students applaud. © Appleton Post Crescent—*USA TODAY Network.*

Four turned their backs to Wallace and folded their arms when he entered.[533] In the midst of his typical discussion of law and order, forty Black students from the campus Afro-American Association stood up and walked out to the applause of several white students, briefly interrupting Wallace's remarks. After Wallace supporters were allowed in to fill the vacant seats, Wallace attacked busing as an artificial way of achieving educational opportunity, saying that he favored freedom of choice and that the college students would understand why people opposed busing when they were parents.[534] Later, he responded to the silent treatment and walkout tersely: "People have the right to respond the way they want to."[535]

MILKING COWS AND SOUTH SIDE VOTES

When in the Dairy State, do as the Dairy Staters do, Wallace must have thought on his visit to a Watertown dairy farm. After briefing the candidate on the price of milk and farming issues, one of the farmers, Milton Piper, pledged support for Wallace because he was "fed up with high taxes and thought Governor Wallace would provide relief."[536] Wallace mounted the counter of the dairy store and, speaking to one hundred people, denounced high taxes and promised tax breaks for farmers by cutting government spending and unfair tax loopholes, before eating cheese, drinking milk and going for a ride on a snowmobile.[537]

Gonzo journalist Hunter S. Thompson covered Wallace's primary campaign in his journalistic cult classic, *Fear and Loathing on the Campaign Trail, '72*. Satirically mocking the polluted Lake Michigan, the city's obsession with sausage and sauerkraut and his shock at being chastised for jaywalking in the streets of a midwestern city, Thompson covered Wallace's campaign from a "dungeon of a hotel" in downtown Milwaukee.[538] Thompson attended Wallace's return to Serb Hall, the scene of the dramatic and racially charged confrontation during his 1964 campaign. According to the journalist, the rally was added last minute to Wallace's schedule and was full of "Polish factory workers just getting off of work."[539] He was fed free beer, as were all other "guests," and interviewed Wallace supporters. One said he was indifferent to politics prior, but Wallace appealed to him since he "comes right out and just says it" and didn't beat around the bush. Thompson described the scene as "electric," and six minutes into Wallace's speech, Thompson quipped, "I had a sense that the bastard had somehow levitated himself and was hovering over us. It reminded me of a Janis Joplin concert."[540] While he

After visiting a dairy farm, Wallace rides a snowmobile with a supporter. *AP photo/Paul Shane.*

was skeptical prior to the night at Serb Hall, he understood Wallace's appeal by the end of the night: "He jerked this crowd in Serb Hall around like he and them all on wires. They were laughing, shouting whacking each other on the back…it was a flat-out fire and brimstone *performance*."[541]

The scene in 1972 was less confrontational than eight years earlier. Peppered in the crowd of six hundred was the occasional picket—one read, "Bigots are blabbermouths."[542] At Serb Hall, Wallace touted low property taxes in his home state and railed against bureaucrats who enabled "welfare loafers" to take federal taxpayer money.[543] Social critic Michael Novak followed the Wallace campaign throughout the state. While he called the rallies "exhausting and exciting…as a championship basketball game," he did not believe that Wallace was a serious threat to win the presidency. Still, he warned that Wallace had tapped into anger among the ethnic working class, who believed they were "besieged by change."[544]

After Serb Hall, a worn-out Wallace attended a nighttime rally in Racine, drawing a crowd of over two thousand. Wallace stumbled over statistics and appeared to be going through the motions, according to the *Milwaukee Journal*, though the *Racine Journal Times* pointed out that it was the largest rally in the city since Wallace last visited four years earlier.[545] Wallace again got the loudest cheers for his opposition to taxation but also mentioned that Wisconsin should be on the lookout for the busing issue, caused by "some social scheming planner [who] doesn't want the average man to exercise control over where his children go to school."[546]

The next day, Wallace was off to a private luncheon in Superior, followed by Eau Claire, where 1,800 supporters, mostly working class, warmly welcomed him with rebel yells in the Memorial High School gym.[547] He attacked the federal income tax as regressive and

Wallace supporters welcomed the governor back to Wisconsin. © Milwaukee Journal-Sentinel—*USA TODAY Network.*

property taxes as too high.[548] According to one local paper, "Archie Bunker would have loved him."[549]

The Saturday before the primary, Wallace was up north in Marshfield, Rhinelander and Wausau, filled with "obvious regret that time might cut short what his staff sees as a swelling of popular support" for the primary only three days away.[550] Privately, he said that some extra time in the Badger State would have gone a long way to shore up support that would have helped his campaign send a resounding message in the Midwest after his stunning victory in Florida. He spoke to over two thousand "adherents, the curious, and a smattering of anti-Wallace demonstrators" at the Armory in Marshfield.[551] The Memorial building in Rhinelander was filled with 750 people who were "cool" but still generally receptive. Two hecklers booed Wallace until Alabama troopers escorted them out of the facility. Wausau East High School had an overflow crowd of nearly 1,800—again, mostly receptive, with a few young people jeering in the back of the Auditorium.[552] Among his normal talking points, Wallace retorted, "Fifty years from now the American people are going to look back and say, 'how callous could the American government have been'" in response to busing and taxation.[553]

Wallace concluded his primary run with stops in Fond du Lac and Sheboygan. He spoke to 200 at the Rotary Club in Fond du Lac, attacking the "remoteness of the [federal] government from the people and the remoteness of the Democratic Party from the people."[554] Wallace concluded his campaign at a rally of more than 3,400 at the Sheboygan Armory. The rally did not end on a high note for the governor, however, as "Wallace was shaken by boos and catcalls from a large contingent of young people in the

Protestors mock Wallace as a racist by dressing up in Ku Klux Klan robes at his final rally in Sheboygan. © Sheboygan Press—*USA TODAY Network*.

balcony," losing his place and becoming distracted by protesters parading down the aisles in Klan robes.[555] One protester attempted to hang a sign reading "Wallace is a Fascist," over the balcony, but a Wallace supporter tore it down. Over 400 "boisterous high school and college age youths got up from their seats and walked out of the armory—arms raised and fists clenched toward Wallace."[556] A flustered Wallace concluded his speech, making a pitch to support him to send a message and lower taxes, arguing that "lower taxes mean more money in the consumer's pocket," which would lead to more jobs and less poverty.[557] Though the protesters were loud, Wallace supporters fired back with equal intensity, giving Wallace a vocal sendoff at the end of his campaign.[558] According to the *Sheboygan Press*, the rowdiness and disorder of the Sheboygan speech was a "fitting climax to the raucous campaign waged in Wisconsin."[559]

Another Surprise on Election Night

With his whirlwind tour and late surge, Wallace ended up finishing strong in second place with nearly a quarter of the primary vote, winning over 22 percent of voters with only a week of campaigning. Despite his second-place showing, however, Wallace struggled with complexities of delegate rules, which were awarded by winning congressional districts, and so he ended up winning no delegates from Wisconsin.[560]

As he did in 1964, Wallace took a loss and claimed victory, declaring himself a "viable candidate."[561] Claiming he only expected to get around 9 percent of the vote, Wallace expressed regret that he spent only eight days in Wisconsin. Watching returns from his motel headquarters in Milwaukee, Wallace claimed a "victory for average citizens of our country."[562] Wallace was aided by significant Republican crossover in the primary vote, as the Democratic voter turnout was four times that of the essentially uncontested Republican contest (it typically was closer to 50–50).[563] The party crossover clouded major takeaways or analysis that could be drawn from the primary, muddling the field going forward.[564]

Still, many Wisconsinites were forced to grapple with another jolt from Wallace. As one editor put it, "Many more voters than we suspected sincerely voted for Wallace because they believed in him."[565] Some worried that the vote shamed the Badger State by "turning a demagogue and racist into a real presidential contender."[566] Another paper lamented the strong showing for Wallace, noting that he "slickly promised answers for everything and solutions to almost nothing."[567]

As a result of his good showing, Wallace ramped up efforts in other northern primaries.[568] Interestingly, his campaign continued to advertise in Wisconsin papers, soliciting financial support to cover television and radio advertising.[569]

Reaction to Wallace's Campaign and Visits

Wallace, as he did the previous two races, tapped into white, working-class supporters who turned out for his rallies and backed him in the press. One middle-aged housewife wearing homemade Wallace earrings, Marie Ryon, attended Wallace's kickoff rally in Milwaukee. Despite not being able to hear him over the cheering, she said, "It doesn't make any difference. Anything he says is true. You just know he's telling the truth."[570] Another supporter in the crowd, electrician Joe Dreblow, claimed that liberal Democrats in Washington "lost contact with the mainstream of American life."[571] Still other supporters on hand were interviewed and claimed Wallace "speaks for the people" and "will do what he says."[572]

Though Wallace got a frigid reception at the event at Lawrence University, a few students left thinking that Wallace was "really cool" and charismatic.[573] A student at New Berlin Eisenhower High School backed Wallace, stating that all the other candidates "are like clumps of seaweed going with the tide."[574] One paper noted that Wallace events attracted many blue-collar women, "who tend to let their husbands and sons do the shouting at the rallies."[575] One article found a sizable pocket of support for Wallace in Union Grove. Supporters included Republicans who planned to cross over in the primary but vote for Nixon in the general election. Another said that the others "had their chance," and yet another thought Wallace "struck a chord" with his stance on taxation.[576] One member of the Dane County Republican Caucus defected to support Wallace.[577] In Wausau, a "Citizens for Wallace" group formed to "bring the nation in accord with the principles laid down by our Founding Fathers."[578] A widowed waitress planned to back Wallace because he "tells it like it is" and "makes sense" on taxes.[579] A Black Vietnam War veteran named James Peters pledged to support Wallace "so we could get to fighting and stop the jiving," arguing that less talk and more fighting was needed to "get this country straightened around."[580] An industrial worker named Edmund Marszalek planned to support Wallace because "the quiet people have taken too much. It's a lousy government I fought for once, but I wouldn't again."[581]

An editorial in the *Portage Daily Register* and *Chippewa Herald Telegram* called on the other candidates to "forget about Wallace," arguing that bringing him attention gave his campaign oxygen and wasted the time and resources of the other campaigns.[582] An angry Wisconsinite, apparently misunderstanding the letter, wrote to the *Herald Telegram* and encouraged voters to forget the two-party system and back Wallace.[583]

An editorial in the *Fox Lake Representative* seemed to defend Wallace by blasting busing as "racism in reverse," arguing that busing is a "lousy method" of solving the issue and that "bigotry is eliminated by teaching a child to love and respect their fellow man."[584]

One letter to the editor explained support for Wallace as a reaction of working people against elitism.[585] Another denied race played a role in Wallace's popularity; rather his populist beliefs and opposition to taxes helped him garner support.[586] Wallace was a man of principles and had the best "horse sense" of any of the candidates, according to another letter.[587]

'Lemme Do fo' You What Ah've Done fo' the Alabama Worker!'

Wallace regularly attacked the *Milwaukee Journal* and other papers for covering his campaign unfairly. Political cartoons critical of Wallace recurred over his first three campaigns. © Milwaukee Journal-Sentinel—*USA TODAY Network*.

Another argued that Wallace listened to the people on issues like busing, unlike other leaders, who didn't heed their concerns.[588] One person wrote to complain about unflattering pictures of Wallace that were used by the *Milwaukee Journal*, an apparent example of bias against the governor, while another did not appreciate a "hogwash" piece in the *Racine Journal Times* that covered Wallace unflatteringly.[589] Another supporter believed he was the only serious candidate committed to "arresting the advance of the welfare state," supporting "the dignity of man" and "upholding the Constitution."[590] Another blasted the news media for not giving Wallace a chance, claiming he was a "down to earth, spokesman for the truly underprivileged, needlessly overburdened taxpayers."[591] A Beloit man admired Alabama's lower tax burden and argued that Wallace "will be his own man" as president.[592] Angered at accusations of Wallace's bigotry, one couple wrote to the *Journal* saying that "if you are a bigot when you defend the common hard working taxpaying man who no longer has a say about his government or how his tax money is spent or what type of education his children get…then believe us we are bigots and very proud of it."[593]

Although the opposition was not as vehement, Wallace found protesters and opponents at most of his stops in Wisconsin. The other primary candidates alternated between condemning and ignoring Wallace. Humphrey, who was considered the frontrunner during much of the primary, chastised Wallace for his empty rhetoric supporting the workingman and on taxation.[594] Jackson tried to distance himself from Wallace by drawing distinctions, namely, "For one thing, I am a Democrat."[595] McGovern rejected the notion that Wallace was the "little man's champion."[596] Some McGovern supporters clad in white Klan sheets picketed one of Wallace's stops.[597]

In a crowded field, the press had some editorials and letters to the editor critical of Wallace. The *Wisconsin State Journal* noted sardonically that every night on the campaign Wallace was "attending revival-like hoedowns" that spent more time making people feel good than covering substantive issues.[598] The *Milwaukee Journal* condemned a vote for Wallace as "a wasted vote as well as a vote for divisiveness and bigotry."[599] The *Capital Times* offered an entire spread laying out Wallace's abysmal record as Alabama governor on taxes, law and order, education and public services.[600] Columnist John Wyngaard, calling Wallace a "combative, clever and cynical man," warned that the splintered primary vote could propel Wallace to an embarrassing victory.[601]

The *Oshkosh Northwestern* criticized Wallace, not for being racist, but for being an opportunist playing on people's emotions for political gain.[602] In a campy piece, Bob Woessner wrote sarcastically that people should stop worrying about Wallace embarrassing Wisconsin by winning, since the state was already infamous for McCarthy. He then went through the last four men to become president and how they left the office in shambles, concluding by saying it might be all right to "give a demagogue a chance."[603] The *Milwaukee Journal* reminded readers that Wallace referred to northerners as "lesser breeds" because they were "full of Poles, Italians and Germans."[604] Columnist Gerald Kloss, writing a long topical poem, included, "But on one thing they all agree—George Wallace ain't the man for me!"[605] The *Capital Times* attacked Wallace's campaign as trying to "sell southern-fried racism under the guise of a populist crusade."[606] The *Milwaukee Journal* pointed out that in Wallace's Alabama, murder rates were high, workers' rights were poor, taxation was broken and education was substandard.[607]

A letter to the editor blasted Wallace's record on taxation, education and law and order in Alabama, accusing Wallace of using hate and fear to divide.[608] Another branded Wallace a "racist demagogue" who kept Black children from integrating in his state.[609] A student from La Crosse criticized Wallace, saying he provided no plan or details to address the problems he laid out.[610]

Union leaders, worried about Wallace's support, conducted internal polls and gave speeches trying to dissuade rank-and-file support for the Alabamian.[611] Wallace clearly intended to tap into union support, bringing Alabama workers on the campaign tour, hanging banners that pledged union support and peppering his support from Alabama workers into his speeches. The Wisconsin AFL-CIO prepared 250,000 leaflets that were meant to warn members of his anti-union record.[612] An ad found in papers across the state warned members that "a vote for Wallace counts for Nixon in '72!"[613] UAW leadership called Wallace "blatantly racist" but planned no campaign to defeat his candidacy.[614]

Wisconsin politicians avoided attacking Wallace directly but saw him as a threat. Senator Gaylord Nelson predicted crossover votes would help Wallace crack the top three in the primary.[615] Democratic governor Lucey vowed to refrain from any endorsements in the primary but privately had concerns about Wallace and vowed to intervene only if it appeared the Alabamian would win.[616] He hinted at Wallace in a speech, saying, "You'd think the whole issue of property taxes was invented by the governor of Alabama."[617] Congressman Zablocki, seen as "the dean of Wisconsin Democrats in Congress" also declined to weigh in on the primary race.[618]

Others warned that Wallace's support was stronger than it appeared. The editor of the *Atlanta Constitution* cautioned journalism students at UW-Milwaukee that many voters claiming to be undecided were likely Wallace supporters who were too ashamed to publicly declare their allegiance to the controversial candidate.[619] Political scientists at the University of Wisconsin analyzed polling and predicted Wallace would receive substantial support from Republicans crossing over in the open primary.[620] Leaders of the Democratic Party worried that Wallace's momentum would lead to party disunity and could spur another run as an independent, hurting the party's chances against Nixon.[621]

Black Wisconsinites' Response to Wallace

Black activists, as they had done in 1964 and 1968, did show up to events in Milwaukee, Lawrence University and elsewhere, but they were not nearly as loud, disruptive and coordinated as they had been in the previous two campaigns. The era of direct action had ended in Milwaukee, and marching, picketing and large public protests were not responses of the Black community to Wallace.

That did not mean that Wallace's 1972 campaign went unnoticed by Black Wisconsinites. Vel Phillips began lecturing at the University of Wisconsin–Milwaukee in the Department of African American Culture in 1970. In her course Introduction to African American Politics, Phillips blasted Wallace as an "anti-black candidate." Phillips told her classes, "The day hasn't come for George C. Wallace to conduct a campaign strictly on law and order…as always he is using the same old prejudice[d] tactics he has always used."[622]

The Milwaukee NAACP attacked the busing stances of both Nixon and Wallace, saying that refusing to enforce judicial rulings on busing were akin to annulling "judicial enforcement of the 14th amendment," denying equal rights and due process.[623] Chapter president Thomas D. Malone compared Nixon's busing moratorium to the infamous *Dred Scott* decision and worried that such a policy would reestablish the "separate but equal" doctrine. Malone made no endorsements, arguing that busing had no bearing on the Wisconsin primary, but hoped that voters would reject "the candidate from Georgia [he meant Alabama] that we by no means favor."[624]

After their walkout during Wallace's visit to Lawrence University, Black students on campus used the event as a vehicle to express concerns about racism on campus. After the event, the head of a Afro-American Student Association released a statement stating that the walkout was not just "against Alabama hillbillies" or Appleton Wallace backers but against "racism that permeates Lawrence University."[625] Pointing to a lack of Black professors, administrators and courses, Black students argued that more than lip service by students and the university was needed to address racism.[626]

The Black press spent less time on Wallace than they had in either 1964 or 1968. There was no mention of Wallace's campaign stops in Wisconsin explicitly or when he was in town. Consistent with the end of the era of direct action, there were no mentions of rallies, events or protests against the governor.

Issues relevant to the campaign, including busing and desegregation of schools, were mentioned regularly but often without direct mention of

Wallace. For example, an article called "Busing, a Phony Issue" covered the inadequate policy of "intact" busing in the city, in which entire classes of all Black students were transported to an all-white school but did not come into contact with any white students and were kept separate. The article argues that this system was not beneficial to inner-city kids, and despite orders to desegregate, Black students benefitted most from community and neighborhood schools.[627]

There was some mention of the various candidates in the election, and Wallace was covered in these as an obvious non-choice or an afterthought. In "The Rose Report," Clinton Rose weighed the thirteen Democratic candidates, praising Shirley Chisholm for her courage in running (though he saw her chances of winning as "remote") and pointing out strengths, weaknesses and disappointments with McGovern, Humphrey, Muskie and Lindsay. When it came to George Wallace, Rose believed the vote would be useful in identifying "the number of bigots in our midst."[628] He also worried that he would have notably more support from the Black community, which Rose said would "give some idea of the fools in our state."[629]

George, who would have thought in 1968 the school bus would

BRING US TOGETHER?'

The *Milwaukee Star* did not mention Wallace much in 1972, but this cartoon mocks his busing stance. *Provided by the* Milwaukee Courier.

The *Milwaukee Courier* published an article reporting that the Southern Christian Leadership Conference head Dr. Ralph Abernathy had endorsed Shirley Chisholm. Abernathy gave other candidates grades ranging from incomplete (since they kept changing their stances on busing) to Bs for "good men" Lindsay and McGovern. Wallace earned a D "for drop out."[630]

The only time that Wallace came up in more than a passing way was in the March 25 issue of the *Milwaukee Courier*. There is a large political cartoon of Wallace and Nixon flashing peace signs in front of a bus. The caption reads, "George, who would have thought in 1968 the school bus would bring us together," a reference to both candidates' opposition to busing as a means of desegregating schools.[631] Beneath the cartoon was a small blurb about how busing helped Wallace and Nixon do well in Florida, and both were hoping that the issue had "not run out of gas" in Wisconsin. It stated that both candidates knew that busing was not a big issue in Wisconsin and that they would try to make it one unless voters realized and understood that it was a nonissue. The paper pledged to educate readers about all things busing, jokingly starting with the Greyhound bus schedule from Milwaukee to Montgomery.[632]

While the Black response was significantly less than past elections, protesters, leaders and the press still found ways, direct and indirect, of asserting their opposition to his states' rights policies. Black Wisconsinites' demand for equal protection had become more muted but was still present in the 1972 campaign.

Momentum Disrupted by Milwaukee Assassin

Wallace went on to win surprising first-place victories in primary elections in Maryland and Michigan, but not before a Wisconsinite brought the Alabamian's campaign to a screeching halt. Milwaukeean Arthur Bremer, a young man from an abusive family who was described as odd and reserved by his neighbors and peers, began stalking both Wallace and Nixon, determined to assassinate one of them to prove his manliness to a former girlfriend who spurned him. Bremer volunteered with the Wallace campaign and attended rallies in Wisconsin to get close to the governor, but he was never able to carry out his attempt. He briefly stalked Nixon on a trip to Ottawa, Canada, before deciding that Wallace was a more realistic target. Bremer followed Wallace to Michigan and Maryland, before shooting the governor three times on a campaign stop in Maryland, paralyzing him and confining him to a wheelchair for the rest of his life.[633]

Wallace exited the campaign shortly thereafter, and the Democrats nominated liberal George McGovern, whose momentum swing began with his first-place finish in Wisconsin. While Democrats would give Wallace a slot to speak at the nominating convention, he appeared weak and tired, lacking the populist fire for which he was known. Despite not getting the conservative Wallace's endorsement as he had hoped, Nixon won reelection in a landslide. His successful Southern Strategy allowed for a dominant performance in the traditionally southern Democratic stronghold by embracing a lighter version of Wallace's views on busing and patriotism.[634] Wallace would return to Alabama to his role as governor, but he still had one more chapter to be written in Wisconsin politics.

1976 PRESIDENTIAL CAMPAIGN, DENOUEMENT

Deferred Dreams Realized and an End of an Era in Wisconsin

Although the civil rights movement in Milwaukee had ended for all intents and purposes, the Black community continued to grow and unrealized goals of the movement came to fruition. Vel Phillips would fight for inner core issues on the common council until 1971, when she was appointed to the judiciary, becoming the state's first Black female judge.[635] Father Groppi would continue to fight for causes, opposing the Vietnam War and supporting human rights issues locally and nationally.[636]

Right as the 1976 primary was underway in Wisconsin, after nearly a decade of litigation, Judge John Reynolds (the governor who opposed Wallace during the 1964 primary election) ruled that Milwaukee Public Schools must desegregate. The same year, the state legislature passed Chapter 220, creating state funding for school districts that accepted students from the city of Milwaukee.[637]

The Final Campaign

Wallace claimed to have a "racial epiphany" following his crippling assassination attempt, softening his stance on segregation and race in the final stage of his political career. Some critics argued this was nothing more than a pragmatic attempt to win the Black voter base, while others believed that his emotional and physical pain helped him empathize with the suffering of others.[638] While this introspection about the wrongheadedness of trampling on the rights of poor and vulnerable Black people may have been genuine, it must be noted that his change of heart did not happen on Bloody Sunday or in the schoolhouse door when there would have been a political cost, but rather when it was politically expedient. Still, the governor's revisionist claim was that he opposed segregation merely because he "was against big government," not due to race.[639]

Wallace ran for and won reelection as Alabama governor in 1974, remarkably winning nearly a third of the Black vote.[640] He had also separated from his wife, Cornelia, which devolved into a messy public affair.[641] Despite personal misgivings about a grueling campaign with tenuous health, Wallace announced his candidacy for president for a fourth and final time in 1975.

Wallace believed he could win the party's nomination and refused to be seen as a "circus act." In his final act, the Alabamian was "bound and determined to turn respectable—if that was the only way he could have the nomination."[642] But his move to moderate his positions failed to generate the raucous throngs of supporters that were a staple of his previous campaigns.[643]

Other factors complicated Wallace's last hurrah. There was a competitive primary on the Republican side, with Ronald Reagan and Gerald Ford fighting for the GOP nomination. This made crossover votes harder to come by. Additionally, his main opponent on the Democratic side was Jimmy Carter, who was running in Wallace's lane as a southerner and Washington outsider.[644]

Wallace continued to blast the federal government, promising to a National Lieutenant Governor's Association that if he were elected it would be "trimmed down and government [would be] taken out of their lives.[645] While Wallace continued to accuse the federal government of being unresponsive to the average man, Jody Carlson pointed out, Wallace's zeal was gone and "in his attempt to create a more respectable image, Wallace [had] become less defiant; the passion [was] no longer there."[646] Wallace continued to rail against busing, ironically arguing that a program designed to establish equality denied people their basic rights.[647] He claimed that states' rights were crucial as a "check against the massive power of the federal government's uncaring bureaucracy....Rights of the state are sacred and should not be tampered" by Washington.[648]

Wallace's dominance of southern politics, however, was loosening as he faced Georgia governor Jimmy Carter in the Democratic primaries.

Wallace was confined to his wheelchair during his abbreviated 1976 campaign in Wisconsin. He had Secret Service detail after he was shot and nearly assassinated four years earlier. Wisconsin State Journal *image by Roger Turner, reprinted with permission.*

Wallace's defeats in the Florida and North Carolina primaries to Jimmy Carter imperiled his presidential campaign prior to the Wisconsin primary.[649] Wallace had only two reporters traveling with his campaign as he headed back to Wisconsin one final time.

FISHING FOR SUPPORT AT SERB HALL

Before stepping foot in the Badger State, it was apparent that Wallace's campaign was in trouble. He fired his country western band that had energized his rallies four years earlier, as well as over thirty campaign workers.[650] His campaign strategy had also changed from previous runs in Wisconsin. Due to lack of funds, Wallace would not hold the huge raucous rallies that had been a staple of his success but would focus more on television, newspaper and radio interviews. Wallace said the change was because the media "doesn't show anything but my wheelchair," but a campaign manager later admitted that the cost played a large role. While rallies were simply preaching to the choir, media interviews could reach a broader audience.[651] During the primary, Wallace flew to Washington for an interview on *Meet the Press*. During the interview, he predicted a win in Wisconsin, citing his appeal among the farmers and workers of the state. He also announced that this would be his final run for president.[652]

Wallace also faced a challenge that he had not had in either of his other primary campaigns in Wisconsin: a competitive Republican primary on the other side. President Gerald Ford faced stiff competition from conservative California governor Ronald Reagan. Conservative Republicans were not as likely to cross over to the Democratic primary, which had been a key ingredient to Wallace's successes in 1964 and 1972.

When Wallace returned to Milwaukee on March 26, his talking points remained largely the same, but much had changed. Wallace appeared to be moderating his stances on a number of issues (opposing welfare cheats, but not welfare as a whole for example), and without the raucous rallies and with his campaign on life support, his fire and passion that drew supporters in were diminished.[653] He began his campaign with a news conference at a Milwaukee hotel blocks away from Arthur Bremer's former home, pledging that despite his setbacks, he was still a serious candidate.[654] Brushing off concerns with his health, Wallace said the real issue was big government and "too much regulation."[655] The Reynolds ruling forcing the desegregation of Milwaukee Public Schools gave Wallace fodder to resurrect a key issue from four years earlier: busing. The *Wisconsin State Journal* argued that Wallace's opponent in the 1964 primary might have helped him again with the decision, bringing the issue of busing into the realm of possibility.[656] In a response to a Milwaukee reporter, a sarcastic Wallace feigned surprise, "You mean you have segregation here? Twelve years ago I was told we had segregation and you didn't. We have integrated schools in Alabama."[657] Wallace hedged by saying he supported integration of schools but opposed illegal and artificial federal efforts to achieve integration through busing. He said he supported a constitutional amendment to allow freedom of choice in education, calling for "nondiscrimination" in assigning people to schools based on choice not skin color.[658]

Wallace began the campaign at a fish fry at Serb Hall, the south side venue that had offered him raucous support in 1964 and 1972. One of his Democratic challengers, Arizona congressman Mo Udall, showed up prior to the rally to meet dinner patrons and shake hands. Days earlier, he had made critical remarks about Wallace, and the Alabamian's supporters in the hall jeered and heckled Udall, shouting, "Go home, Mo!"[659] When Wallace finally took the stage at Serb Hall, he had around five hundred supporters on hand for the homecoming, cheering, "Wallace, Yes!, Busing, No!"[660] Saying he felt at home and spoke the language of the south side, he opposed "forced busing" and called for freedom of choice in schooling, arguing, "Let the parent or guardian of each child send them where they want to send them."[661] He followed up with an attack on the federal government, "Let the people make the decisions without some federal judge making it for them."[662] On desegregation, Wallace joked, "I was on your side before you were on my side," describing the lack of northern support for southern opposition to desegregation efforts.[663] Wallace focused on "middle-class issues," including taxation, inflation and unemployment, again reciting Alabama's low tax rates and railing against welfare cheaters and foreign aid. He worried that the "middle class is being destroyed by runaway inflation and the tax load."[664] He also resurrected his "law and order" rhetoric, blasting leniency on criminals and calling to "put 'em in the electric chair!"[665] Supporters cheered Wallace throughout his speech, often shouting, "Right on!"[666] One supporter wore a red, white and blue suit and top hat covered with a dozen Wallace pins and stickers and with a picture of the governor embroidered on his breast pocket.[667] Unlike his previous events at the Milwaukee Auditorium and Serb Hall, there were no reported protesters, pickets or disruptions.

The next day, the governor met around one hundred people at his campaign office on National Avenue in Milwaukee. Wallace signed

Wallace supporters cheer at one last rally at Serb Hall. © Milwaukee Journal-Sentinel—USA TODAY Network.

autographs, shook hands and gave a pep talk to his campaign staffers, posing for photographs with supporters, including a small boy and his delighted dad.[668] After encouraging staff and supporters that they could carry the state, one woman told the governor, "We need you. We really need you," as he signed her hat.[669]

Trip Cut Short after "Shameful" Protest

Wallace resumed his campaign on Monday March 29, flying into La Crosse and then to Green Bay for more radio and television interviews, which allowed his fledgling campaign "to provide maximum exposure at minimum cost."[670] Throughout the campaign, Wallace accused his opponents of stealing ideas that he had popularized in his previous campaigns. "They all stole my issues," Wallace accused. "Now they are all drawing water out of the same well."[671] Again deflecting concerns about his health, Wallace quipped, "At least I am not paralyzed in the head [like] some of the people that have been running our government."[672] Wallace complained the media spent too much time focusing on the wheelchair and claimed that he was a healthy man, spitting back, "I just had an accident. I was shot. I don't have a disease."[673]

Upon his return from Washington, Wallace's first event in Wisconsin was a TV appearance on an Easter Seals telethon. He did an interview with the *La Crosse Tribune*, spending a large portion discussing how to reduce American dependence on foreign agricultural products, supporting quotas to limit the impact on Wisconsin farmers.[674] Again complaining about how "gluttonous" big government had become, Wallace railed against the Department of Health, Education and Welfare and reiterated his opposition to busing.[675] He held a brief press conference in the city, but the *La Crosse Tribune* noted the absence of a rambunctious rally as had occurred four years earlier. The paper blamed the wheelchair for changing his "style," and other than a line of well-wishers that he greeted upon his arrival, his visit was without incident.[676]

Later that day, he arrived at Austin Straubel Airport in Green Bay as a dozen supporters met him with flags and held another press conference. Blasting his opponents as "Johnny-come-latelies" and downplaying his cancelation of rallies in favor of press conferences and interviews, Wallace stressed his second-place position in the delegate count as evidence that he was a competitive candidate.[677] He then hosted around one hundred people at a "public open house," claiming credit for other candidates joining him in calling for the "federal government [to get] off of the people's backs." Wallace saw two groups during a two-hour open house, not pausing for reaction and receiving polite applause only at the end of his statements.[678] Though he remained upbeat, a poll showed him in last place of the four Democratic candidates, with only 15 percent of the state's vote.[679] The *Milwaukee Journal* noted the small crowds at his public appearances in Green Bay were a stark "contrast to his frenzied emotional rallies" of his previous campaigns.[680] When asked by a Green Bay reporter about the lack of enthusiasm in his campaign, Wallace claimed that he didn't "raise my voice as much" since most of campaign was over television interviews.[681]

Wallace appeared in Madison on Monday to do more television interviews and held his second rally of the campaign at the Cuba Club. The *Capital Times* had harsh words for his campaign visit, noting that despite the usual jibes, the "epithets…sound stale and tired" because his ideas had been coopted more politely by his rivals and because the man himself was a "gray facsimile of the cocky little fighter he used to be."[682] In an interview with the *Capital Times*, Wallace bristled at the notion that Carter represented a "New South," and when told that the paper had already endorsed one of his rivals, Morris Udall, Wallace quipped that the paper may "change its mind" after the interview.[683] Still, the interviewer described him as a "shrunken" man who knew the campaign was over.[684] Irritated that the image of the schoolhouse door had stuck all of these years, Wallace claimed, "We've moved past that" and that he was never against the people but "big government."[685]

Wallace's speech at a luncheon for the Optimists Club at the Cuba Club was the only one of the 1976 campaign that attracted protesters. Around ten student activists mocked the governor by wearing masks of his would-be assassin's face, Arthur Bremer, while pushing

Wallace's campaign was subdued in 1976 and lacked the intense, passionate rallies of his earlier candidacies. Here he is meeting with the media in a small event. Wisconsin State Journal *image by Roger Turner, reprinted with permission.*

Protesters in Madison mock Wallace by wearing masks of his would-be assassin and carting around wheelchairs. *From the* Capital Times, *reprinted with permission.*

around empty wheelchairs.[686] They shouted callously for Wallace to "stand up for the issues," and "free Artie Bremer [who was in jail for sixty-three years because of his attempted assassination], give him another chance! He should have shot him in the head, but he shot him in the pants!"[687] One demonstrator got into the Cuba Club and marched around chanting before the Secret Service removed him. Ignoring the demonstrators, Wallace gave a speech that attacked his opponents as copycats and railed on the well-worn issues of his campaign: taxation, welfare, bureaucracy and busing. He had words for "some of you folks at the University of Wisconsin," claiming to have won 95 percent of the support in counties that were primarily Black. Wallace fired, "You can't beat that, even if you count 'em yourself."[688]

The speech itself barely made a dent in the press coverage, but the protesters sparked widespread outrage and a slew of public remarks and apologies from elected officials, including Democratic Governor Lucey, who apologized on behalf of the state and blasted the protesters for their insensitivity.[689] Wallace brushed off the apologies, saying he did not "want any sympathy" and that he was an able man.[690] He said no apology was necessary as the people of Wisconsin had been good to him over the years and brushed off the protesters as "kooks."[691] While Wisconsin senator William Proxmire also denounced the protests, Madison mayor Paul Soglin refused to apologize because Wallace has never apologized for blocking Black students from attending schools in his state.[692]

END OF THE ROAD

Following the fireworks in Madison, Wallace traveled to Janesville to be interviewed by a television network there, announcing that he planned to cut his campaign in Wisconsin short to work on the budget in Alabama. He denied it had anything to do with the hecklers, downplaying the incident by saying he wish he could have stood up and he was thankful they didn't throw a firecracker at him.[693] The *New York Times* noted that Wallace has "shaken fewer than 1090 hands, held none of the noisy rallies and has visited no shopping centers or courthouse greens."[694] While in town, he deviated from his campaign tactics, attending a high school assembly, telling around one thousand students that being tough on crime meant "sure and swift punishment with an electric chair."[695] He also stopped at a Wausau motel, speaking briefly to four hundred mostly young people, who greeted him with a warm reception.[696] After spending Wednesday in Eau Claire for a brief press conference, where he believed he had a "lot of support," he traveled to Rhinelander and Racine on Thursday and Superior on Friday before heading back to his home state.[697] In addition to his typical issues, he told a radio station in Rhinelander that the United States needed a better energy policy, calling on more coal, an Alaskan pipeline, investment in solar power and less energy usage to relieve foreign dependence.[698]

As Wallace left Wisconsin on Friday, he offered some parting words at a press conference at the Ramada Inn in Milwaukee, imploring voters to send a message against forced busing. Prior to the conference, he met some factory workers switching shifts at Allen Bradley. Some shouted, "Give 'em hell, George," and others apologized for the Bremer hecklers.[699] In a TV interview, Wallace said that middle-class people were "fed up with big government."[700] As he planned his departure from Wisconsin, his aide pledged that over twenty thirty-minute campaign broadcasts were to air in the state before the election.[701] He predicted he would do well in Wisconsin and vowed to fight on regardless of the results.[702]

From Alabama, Wallace made one last appeal to Wisconsin voters to "put our message in boldface so both parties will have to take notice."[703] Over a phone interview in Montgomery, Wallace predicted success in Wisconsin but failed to speculate on the outcome.[704] An advertisement in the *Sheboygan Press* called for support for Wallace and hoped for a Carter-Wallace ticket to cement moderate and conservative Democratic support.[705]

On election night, Jimmy Carter won a narrow victory in Wisconsin, with Wallace running a distant third place with only 13 percent of the popular vote.[706]

Despite his poor showing, pockets of Wisconsin showed support for Wallace, including Milwaukee's south side (17 percent), northwestern Wisconsin (19 percent) and northeastern Wisconsin (15 percent).[707] While crossover votes certainly helped Wallace in 1964 and 1972, they appeared to be a nonfactor in 1976, with 55 percent voting in the Democratic primary and 45 percent in the Republican primary, a more normal partisan balance.[708] Wallace said he was "elated" to have won ten delegates in Wisconsin and vowed to fight on.[709] However, before the results were done, Wallace reduced his staffing to thirty people, offered to sublease his jet and began canceling appearances, signaling the de facto end of the race.[710] The *Milwaukee Journal* declared that Wallace was "all but eliminated" after another poor showing.[711] The *Milwaukee Sentinel* deemed it a "knock-out punch" for Wallace.[712]

In the end, Carter gained the nomination, partly by coopting Wallace's views, populism and policy positions. Without the fire and by adopting more moderate positions, Wallace was unable to distinguish himself from other candidates, dooming his last chance at the White House.[713]

REACTION TO WALLACE

Despite his presence in the race, Wallace did not attract much attention from the other major candidates. Carter was basically mum on Wallace, and other than Udall saying he "didn't consider Wallace a decent human being," which he quickly retracted, there were almost no attacks on the governor.[714] Governor Lucey, as in 1972, avoided picking a favorite in the primary but named Wallace as the only candidate for governor that he could not endorse.[715] Unlike the previous races, there was no mention of labor getting involved to oppose Wallace's candidacy.

Wallace got less press coverage than any of the previous races, and many papers doubted Wallace had a chance of being a serious candidate. The *Capital Times* noted that on all of Wallace's issues, the issue of race was "prowling around the edges."[716] The *Fond du Lac Reporter* was among the chorus of papers that argued Wallace's campaign "lacked the fire, controversy and issues of previous races."[717]

Many people were uninterested or opposed to Wallace's campaign. The *Racine Journal Times* found lots of negative responses to Wallace, including people saying they weren't interested in talking about him or one Democrat pledging to move to Canada if Wallace was elected.[718] The *Wisconsin Jewish*

Herald interviewed Wallace on his stances on Jewish issues, including Israel and Soviet Jewry.[719]

The most media attention, and strongest support of Wallace, came after the Bremer-masked hecklers. The *Milwaukee Journal* called the protest "disgusting," "uncivilized" and "cruel."[720] The *La Crosse Tribune* branded the protesters as "sick minds" who shamed the state.[721] The *Milwaukee Sentinel* called the protesters "disgusting" and criticized their behavior as subhuman.[722] The U.S. Senate voted unanimously to pass a resolution condemning the "work of a gang of thugs," calling the actions of the Madison protesters "cruel, callous and undemocratic."[723] Despite widespread condemnation and dozens of letters to the editor across the state, the student protesters refused to apologize, saying that although their actions were tasteless, they were justified. They refused to sympathize with Wallace, and the antics were an "attempt to mock his crippled, racist policies."[724]

Wallace, even without the boisterous rallies, found supporters all along the campaign trail. At the Allen Bradley factory, one female worker said he was the "only one who's taken a decent stand on integration," while another noted that only Wallace had bothered to come and meet the working people. Two students, hearing of his appearance at the plant rushed down there, praising Wallace for taking a stand on busing "before that was a popular stand."[725] One letter to the editor praised Wallace's pro-life stance, and called on people to support "a government by the people and the right to life passed on to the future."[726] Another claimed his stances on busing, foreign aid, and taxation made him the "only candidate who speaks for rank and file citizens on all issues."[727] Yet another praised Wallace for warning in 1964 that civil rights was a disguise for government takeover of local government and in 1972 warning about big government and taxation. The author wondered if others who had adopted his stances were sincere.[728] In a Christian radio address, Richard Wolfe praised Wallace and Reagan for adhering to Lincoln's maxim that "he is best who is governed least" and for working to return local control to the people from the federal government.[729] Another letter praised Wallace and Reagan as the "two candidates who deserve the honored conservative designation."[730] A letter to the *Racine Journal Times* praised Wallace for telling it like it is, and not just saying what people want to hear.[731] Another noted that Wallace didn't have labor leaders' support because he wasn't a socialist and didn't have big businesses support because he couldn't be bought. He was a true man of the people.[732]

Black Response to Wallace

In 1976, there was essentially no response to Wallace's campaign by the Black community, a dramatic reversal from twelve years earlier when the governor faced organized and strong resistance. The absence of the Black community in this campaign was likely a result of the nonexistence of public rallies, which had been meeting places of his opponents and supporters. Wallace also was not the vibrant and vocal threat to the Black community that he had been previously, and his campaign had already essentially ended prior to his appearance in Wisconsin. Additionally, the era of direct action reached its height nearly ten years earlier and an organized Black resistance movement had essentially disintegrated by 1976.

At an assembly at Rufus King High School in Milwaukee, Reverend Jesse Jackson called on students to examine the candidates' records and their willingness to take Black people's concerns seriously when crafting policy decisions. Referencing Wallace briefly, Jackson warned that even if the governor was not the Democratic nominee, "his absence could not be called the presence of justice."[733]

The Black press had very little to say about Wallace. The *Milwaukee Courier* took pleasure in finding the man "who stood in the school house door has lost his chance to stand in the White House door" and described his campaign as "mortally wounded." The author criticized Wallace as "the worst of the bigots because he couples his racism with professional political skills" by creating a "system of code words to denigrate Blacks. Noting that Wallace's image had "hovered like a low-hanging storm cloud over the Democratic Party," the author warned that racism was still "very much alive in American politics."[734]

There were a few mentions of Wallace in the presses' effort to get out the vote. The "Rose Report" in the *Milwaukee Star Times* predicted that a large Black voter turnout would be "a major factor in offsetting any thrust that Wallace may have in the state." Warning that unless inner-city voters were jarred from their complacency, there might be no liberal Black allies on the ballot in November.[735] Dismissing Wallace as "out of the question," the *Milwaukee Courier* called on Black voters to support Carter as the "happy medium."[736]

By 1976, the clash between Wallace and his supporters' federalism and the Black communities quest for equal protection had dissipated. Wallace's campaign had become a sideshow, and the Black community barely recognized and responded to the repetitive rhetoric.

Coda

Wallace would be elected governor one more time in 1982 but delegated most decisions and spent most of the time ailing and out of the public eye. He married a country singer names Lisa Taylor in 1981 but divorced six years later after a brief and dysfunctional marriage.[737] He spent the final years of his public life renouncing his segregationist stances, asking forgiveness of Black leaders, and even appointed African Americans to his cabinet and state positions. Suffering from deafness, Parkinson's disease and lingering health issues from the failed assassination, Wallace died in 1998, the "most successful loser" in twentieth-century American politics.[738]

In 1978, Vel Phillips became first Black person elected to statewide office in Wisconsin, serving as attorney general until 1983. Groppi remained active in social justice issues, eventually left the priesthood and became a city bus driver before he died of cancer in 1985, a modest ending for a man at the center of such momentous and tumultuous events in Wisconsin history.[739]

Wallace once told a crowd on a chilly 1964 day that if the "War Between the States had been fought in Wisconsin instead of Virginia, you would have won in a week."[740] The Civil War, of course, was an epic struggle to see if America and its Constitution would survive. Wallace brought a battle over the meaning of the Constitution to Wisconsin in four acts between 1964 and 1976. Wallace and his supporters, whether genuinely or not, pledged a states' rights approach, where civil rights legislation, integration, busing and taxation were all examples of a federal government that had gone too far in disrupting the rights of individuals and the doctrine of local control. Activists, civil rights leaders and African Americans in Wisconsin saw the battle lines differently. They reacted to the Wallace candidacy by demonstrating the importance of a strong federal government in ensuring that equal protection and civil liberties be extended to all Americans.

Wallace's candidacy exposed the fault lines between Wisconsinites and where they stood on these constitutional questions. Others, like former governor Scott Walker, successfully capitalized on these fault lines with his "divide and conquer" tactics. His divisive attack on collective bargaining rights and implementation of stringent voter ID laws led civil rights leader Jesse Jackson to compare Walker to Wallace.[741] As we enter a twenty-first century that pits "Making America Great Again" against the notion that "Black Lives Matter," it is evident that these divisions continue to grow deeper in the state. Wallace told a crowd of south siders at Serb Hall that if he were to ever leave Alabama, he would want to come and live in Wisconsin. In many ways, he's never left.

NOTES

Chapter 1

1. McDonald and Jackson, *Finding Freedom*, 21–37.
2. Ibid., 47–48.
3. Ibid., 119–22.
4. Baker, *Rescue of Joshua Glover*, 136–38, 153–58.
5. Greenhaw, *Watch Out for George Wallace*, 1.
6. Frederick, *Stand Up for Alabama*, 19–24.
7. Carter, *Politics of Rage*, 11.
8. Frederick, *Stand Up for Alabama*, 405.
9. Carter, *Politics of Rage*, 121–23.
10. Ibid., 139.
11. Ibid., 149.
12. Carlson, *George C. Wallace*, 61.
13. Ibid., 150–51.
14. History, "The Civil Rights Act of 1964," https://www.history.com/topics/black-history/civil-rights-act.
15. Carter, *Politics of Rage*, 151–55.
16. Ibid., 173.
17. Ibid., 185–86.
18. Gurda, *Making of Milwaukee*, 358–61.
19. P. Jones, *Selma of the North*, 21–23.

20. Gurda, *Making of Milwaukee*, 363.
21. P. Jones, *Selma of the North*, 29.
22. Ibid., 32–35.
23. Ibid., 34.
24. Ibid., 42–48.
25. Ibid., 48.
26. Ibid., 50.
27. Ibid., 63–65.
28. Ibid., 67.

Chapter 2

29. Gregory, *Southern Diaspora*, 304.
30. Carter, *Politics of Rage*, 198–200.
31. Carlson, *George C. Wallace*, 25–26.
32. Haney, "Wallace in Wisconsin," 262.
33. Leahy, "Polish Reaction to the Civil Rights Movement"; Conway, "White Backlash Reexamined."
34. Carter, *Politics of Rage*, 197.
35. *Capital Times*, February 10, 1964, 8; *Milwaukee Journal* April 2, 1964, 255.
36. *Milwaukee Sentinel*, February 18, 1964, 6.
37. Ibid.
38. *Milwaukee Journal*, April 26, 1964, 257.
39. Ibid.
40. *Milwaukee Journal*, April 26, 1964, 266.
41. *Capital Times*, February 19, 1964, 25.
42. *Wisconsin State Journal*, February 19, 1964, 1.
43. *Portage Daily Register*, February 20, 1964, 5.
44. Ibid.
45. *Portage Daily Register*, February 18, 1964, 2; *Wausau Daily Herald*, February 18, 1964, 5.
46. *Capital Times*, February 19, 1964, 25.
47. Haney, "Wallace in Wisconsin," 261.
48. *Capital Times*, February 19, 1964, 38.
49. *Capital Times*, February 12, 1964, 1.
50. *Capital Times*, February 20, 1964, 1.
51. *Capital Times*, February 19, 1964, 4.
52. *Kenosha News*, February 19, 1964, 2.

53. *Green Bay Press-Gazette*, February 19, 1964, 22.
54. W. Jones, *Wallace Story*, 49.
55. Haney, "Wallace in Wisconsin," 261.
56. Ibid., 262; *Sheboygan Press*, March 3, 1964, 7.
57. W. Jones, *Wallace Story*, 172–73.
58. Ibid., 175.
59. *Capital Times*, March 5, 1964, 1, 5.
60. *Milwaukee Journal*, March 6, 1964, 68.
61. Haney, "Wallace in Wisconsin," 260–61.
62. *Eau Claire Daily Telegram*, March 7, 1964, 1.
63. *Milwaukee Journal* March 7, 1964, 1; *La Crosse Tribune*, March 7, 1964, 1.
64. *Wisconsin State Journal*, March 7, 1964, 1–2.
65. *Milwaukee Sentinel*, March 6, 1964, 8.
66. *Marshfield News-Herald*, March 9, 1964, 13.
67. *Capital Times*, March 10, 1964, 1.
68. *Milwaukee Journal*, March 7, 1964, 1.
69. *Milwaukee Journal*, March 13, 1964, 20.
70. *Milwaukee Journal*, March 7, 1964, 1.
71. *Wisconsin State Journal*, March 6, 1964, 25.
72. *Capital Times*, March 6, 1964, 34.
73. *Milwaukee Journal*, March 9, 1964, 18.
74. *Racine Journal Times*, March 9, 1964, 12.
75. *Green Bay Press-Gazette*, March 10, 1964, 4.
76. *Wisconsin State Journal*, March 10, 1964, 8.
77. *Oshkosh Northwestern*, March 11, 1964, 23.
78. *Milwaukee Journal*, March 15, 1964, 82.
79. *Kenosha News*, March 16, 1964, 4.
80. *Eau Claire Daily Telegram*, March 14, 1964, 4.
81. *Green Bay Press-Gazette*, March 15, 1964, 10.
82. *Wisconsin State Journal*, March 16, 1964, 8.
83. *Eau Claire Daily Telegram*, March 7, 1964, 1.
84. *Milwaukee Journal*, March 8, 1964, 1.
85. Haney, "Wallace in Wisconsin," 264–65.
86. *Appleton Post-Crescent*, March 17, 1964, 1; *Appleton Post-Crescent*, March 18, 1964, 22.
87. *Green Bay Press-Gazette*, March 17, 1964, 1.
88. *Green Bay Press-Gazette*, March 17, 1964, 8.
89. *Appleton Post-Crescent*, March 18, 1964, 22.
90. *Green Bay Press-Gazette*, March 18, 1964, 18.

91. *Neenah News-Record*, March 19, 1964, 1; *Oshkosh Northwestern*, March 19, 1964, 1.
92. *Capital Times*, March 19, 1964, 4; *Green Bay Press-Gazette*, March 19, 1964, 1.
93. *Eau Claire Leader-Telegram*, March 19, 1964, 1; *Milwaukee Journal*, March 19, 1964, 5.
94. *Wisconsin State Journal*, March 19, 1964, 2.
95. W. Jones, *Wallace Story*, 182.
96. Ibid.
97. *Milwaukee Journal*, March 16, 1964, 18.
98. *Milwaukee Sentinel*, March 16, 1964, 13.
99. *Milwaukee Sentinel*, March 19, 1964, 6.
100. *Milwaukee Journal*, March 20, 1964, 22.
101. *Milwaukee Sentinel*, March 21, 1964, 19.
102. *Sheboygan Press*, March 17, 1964, 20; *Sheboygan Press*, March 18, 1964, 64.
103. *Eau Claire Daily Telegram*, March 18, 1964, 4.
104. *Milwaukee Journal*, March 18, 1964, 2.
105. *Marshfield News-Herald*, March 18, 1964, 4.
106. *Capital Times*, March 19, 1964, 1.
107. *Racine Journal Times*, March 19, 1964, 10.
108. *Appleton Post-Crescent*, March 20, 1964, 4.
109. *Green Bay Press-Gazette*, March 20, 1964, 3.
110. *Sheboygan Press*, March 17, 1964, 8.
111. *Appleton Post-Crescent*, March 18, 1964, 22.
112. *Green Bay Press-Gazette*, March 17, 1964, 1; W. Jones, *Wallace Story*, 173.
113. *Oshkosh Northwestern*, March 17, 1964, 1.
114. *Milwaukee Sentinel*, March 19, 1964, 1.
115. *Eau Claire Daily Telegram*, March 18, 1964, 21.
116. *Wisconsin State Journal*, March 20, 1964, 12.
117. *Marshfield News-Herald*, March 21, 1964, 4.
118. *La Crosse Tribune*, March 24, 1964, 2.
119. W. Jones, *Wallace Story*, 198–99.
120. Ibid., 203.
121. *Green Bay Press-Gazette*, March 25, 1964, 2.
122. W. Jones, *Wallace Story*, 208–11; *Kenosha News*, March 24, 1964, 1.
123. *Chippewa Herald-Telegram*, March 28, 1964, 1.
124. *Chippewa Herald-Telegram*, March 28, 1964, 4.
125. Ibid.
126. *Eau Claire Leader-Telegram*, March 28, 1964, 12.
127. *Eau Claire Leader*, March 28, 1964, 1.

128. *Milwaukee Journal*, March 28, 1964, 24.
129. *Appleton Post-Crescent*, March 25, 1964, 13.
130. *Sheboygan Press*, March 26, 1964, 44.
131. *Eau Claire Daily Telegram*, March 27, 1964, 18.
132. *Milwaukee Sentinel*, March 30, 1964, 8.
133. *Milwaukee Sentinel*, March 23, 1964, 11.
134. *Racine Journal-Times*, March 26, 1964, 3.
135. Ibid.
136. *Milwaukee Sentinel*, March 30, 1964, 7.
137. *La Crosse Tribune*, March 22, 1964, 8.
138. *Appleton Post-Crescent*, March 24, 1964, 6.
139. *Eau Claire Leader-Telegram*, March 26, 1964, 6.
140. *Sheboygan Press*, March 26, 1964, 44.
141. *Milwaukee Journal*, March 27, 1964, 14.
142. *Milwaukee Sentinel*, April 3, 1964, 8.
143. *Kenosha News*, March 30, 1964, 4.
144. *Wisconsin State Journal*, March 24, 1964, 4; *La Crosse Tribune*, March 24, 1964, 2.
145. *Eau Claire Daily Telegram*, March 26, 1964, 16.
146. Ibid.
147. *Milwaukee Journal*, March 26, 1964, 16.
148. *Eau Claire Daily Telegram*, April 1, 1964, 17.
149. *Green Bay Press-Gazette*, April 1, 1964, 5.
150. *Wausau Daily Record-Herald*, March 25, 1964, 8.
151. *Appleton Post-Crescent*, March 31, 1964, 2.
152. *Milwaukee Journal*, March 31, 1964, 2; *La Crosse Tribune*, March 31, 1964, 1.
153. *Milwaukee Journal*, April 1, 1964, 2; *Sheboygan Press*, April 1, 1964, 3.
154. *Manitowoc Herald-Times*, April 1, 1964, 1.
155. *Sheboygan Press*, April 1, 1964, 3.
156. *Capital Times*, April 2, 1964, 4.
157. *Green Bay Press-Gazette*, April 2, 1964, 3; *Milwaukee Journal*, April 2, 1964, 1; *Kenosha News*, April 2, 1964, 12.
158. *Milwaukee Sentinel*, April 2, 1964, 7; *Capital Times*, April 3, 1964, 32.
159. *Capital Times*, April 3, 1964, 1; *Wisconsin State Journal*, April 3, 1964, 1.
160. *Wisconsin State Journal*, April 3, 1964, 1.
161. *Milwaukee Journal*, April 4, 1964, 1.
162. *Appleton Post-Crescent*, March 31, 1964, 2.
163. *Milwaukee Journal*, April 4, 64, 1; *Milwaukee Sentinel*, April 4, 1964, 1.
164. *Milwaukee Sentinel*, April 2, 1964, 3.

165. *Capital Times*, March 31, 1964, 2.

166. Ibid.

167. *Milwaukee Sentinel*, April 2, 1964, 1, 2.

168. *Milwaukee Journal*, April 6, 1964, 1; *Kenosha News*, April 6, 1964, 2.

169. W. Jones, *Wallace Story*, 191.

170. *Capital Times*, March 31, 1964, 17.

171. *Milwaukee Sentinel*, April 3, 1964, 1.

172. *La Crosse Tribune*, March 31, 1964, 9.

173. *Appleton Post-Crescent*, April 3, 1964, 2.

174. W. Jones, *Wallace Story*, 224.

175. Ibid.

176. *Wisconsin State Journal*, April 4, 1964, 2.

177. *La Crosse Tribune*, March 31, 1964, 6.

178. *Eau Claire Daily Telegram*, April 2, 1964, 6.

179. *Portage Daily Register*, April 3, 1964, 8.

180. *Milwaukee Journal*, April 4, 1964, 8.

181. *Racine Journal-Times*, April 5, 1964, 10.

182. Ibid., 21.

183. *La Crosse Tribune*, April 6, 1964, 15.

184. *Appleton Post-Crescent*, March 31, 1964, 2.

185. *Milwaukee Sentinel*, March 31, 1964, 8.

186. *Green Bay Press-Gazette*, April 3, 1964, 4.

187. Haney, "Wallace in Wisconsin," 259.

188. Gregory, *Southern Diaspora*, 304.

189. Ibid.

190. Carter, *Politics of Rage*, 208.

191. Haney, "Wallace in Wisconsin," 274.

192. Carlson, *George C. Wallace*, 48–49.

193. Carter, *Politics of Rage*, 209–15.

194. Ibid., 222.

195. "Civil Rights Act of 1964."

Chapter 3

196. Wisconsin State Historical Society, "Black History in Wisconsin," https://www.wisconsinhistory.org/Records/Article/CS502.

197. Brautigam, "Wallace Sees Race Feeling in Wisconsin," 25.

198. *Milwaukee Journal*, March 7, 1964, 1.

199. *Milwaukee Journal*, March 16, 1964, 18.

200. *Milwaukee Journal*, March 25, 1964, 18.

201. *Milwaukee Journal*, March 19, 1964, 1; *New York Times*, March 22, 1964, 52.

202. *Milwaukee Journal*, March 19, 1964, 1; *New York Times*, March 22, 1964, 52.

203. *Milwaukee Sentinel*, March 24, 1964, 2.

204. Haney, "Wallace in Wisconsin," 267.

205. *Milwaukee Sentinel*, March 25, 1964, 1.

206. *Oshkosh Northwestern*, March 25, 1964, 3.

207. Haney, "Wallace in Wisconsin," 268.

208. *Milwaukee Journal*, March 25, 1964, 1; *Oshkosh Northwestern*, March 25, 1964, 3.

209. *Milwaukee Sentinel*, March 25, 1964, 1.

210. *Oshkosh Northwestern*, March 25, 1964, 3.

211. *Green Bay Press-Gazette*, March 25, 1964, 1–2.

212. *Milwaukee Sentinel*, March 25, 1964, 6.

213. CORE poster, CORE Records, Box 1, Folder 7, Miscellaneous, Mississippi, George Wallace and Wisconsin State Conference, 1964. Accessed through UW–Milwaukee March on Milwaukee—Civil Rights History Project.

214. *Milwaukee Star*, March 28, 1964, 10.

215. Ibid.

216. *Racine Journal-Times*, March 29, 1964, 7.

217. *Milwaukee Journal*, April 2, 1964, 1–2.

218. Ibid.

219. Ibid.; *Capital Times*, April 2, 1964, 4.

220. *Milwaukee Journal*, April 2, 1964, 1–2.

221. Ibid.

222. Ibid.

223. *Capital Times*, April 3, 1964, 1, 8; *Wisconsin State Journal*, April 3, 1964, 1; *Wausau Daily Herald*, April 3, 1964, 5.

224. *Milwaukee Journal*, April 4, 1964, 1.

225. Ibid.

226. Ibid.

227. *Milwaukee Star*, April 11, 1964, 2.

228. *Milwaukee Sentinel*, April 5, 1964, 1, 5; *Milwaukee Journal*, April 6, 1964, 1–2; *La Crosse Tribune*, April 6, 1964, 8.

229. *Milwaukee Journal*, April 6, 1964, 1–2.

230. W. Jones, *Wallace Story*, 191.

231. Haney, "Wallace in Wisconsin," 273.

232. W. Jones, *Wallace Story*, 208.
233. *Milwaukee Journal*, March 19, 1964, 2; *Jet Magazine*, April 1964, 53.
234. Ibid.
235. *Milwaukee Journal*, March 19, 1964, 5.
236. *Milwaukee Journal*, April 4, 1964, 1.
237. *Milwaukee Journal*, April 6, 1964, 1–2.
238. *Capital Times*, April 1, 1964, 23.
239. Ibid.
240. *Milwaukee Journal*, March 28, 1964, 3.
241. *Milwaukee Sentinel*, April 1, 1964, 2.
242. *Milwaukee Journal*, March 16, 1964, 18.
243. Haney, "Wallace in Wisconsin," 263.
244. Ibid., 268.
245. Ibid., 263–64.
246. *UWM Post*, April 16, 1964, 1.
247. *Milwaukee Star*, February 22, 1964, 1, 4.
248. Ibid.
249. Ibid.
250. *Milwaukee Star*, March 21, 1964, 4.
251. Ibid.
252. *Milwaukee Star*, March 21, 1964, 5.
253. Ibid.
254. Ibid.
255. *Milwaukee Star*, March 21, 1964, 6.
256. Ibid.
257. *Milwaukee Star*, March 21, 1964, 10.
258. *Milwaukee Star*, April 4, 1964, 1–2.
259. *Milwaukee Star*, April 4, 1964, 3.
260. *Milwaukee Star*, March 22, 1964, 4.
261. *Milwaukee Star*, March 21, 1964, 4.
262. *Chicago Defender*, March 10, 1964, 17.
263. *Chicago Defender*, March 18, 1964, 9.
264. *Chicago Defender*, April 2, 1964, 4.
265. *Chicago Defender*, April 7, 1964, 1.
266. Ibid.
267. *Milwaukee Journal*, March 19, 1964, 2; *Jet Magazine*, April 1964, 53.
268. Papers of the NAACP, Press Release, April 3, 1964, accessed from the Library of Congress.
269. Ibid.

270. *Milwaukee Star*, February 22, 1964, 5.
271. *Milwaukee Star*, March 14, 1964, 1.
272. *Milwaukee Star*, March 21, 1964, 2.
273. *Milwaukee Star*, April 4, 1964, 1.
274. *Oshkosh Northwestern*, March 1, 1964, 8.
275. *Milwaukee Journal*, March 7, 1964, 3.
276. *Milwaukee Star*, March 14, 1964, 1.
277. *Milwaukee Sentinel*, March 10, 1964, 2.
278. *Milwaukee Star*, February 22, 1964, 2.
279. *Wisconsin State Journal*, March 25, 1964, 8.
280. Ibid.
281. Ibid.
282. *Milwaukee Journal*, April 2, 1964, 4.
283. Ibid.
284. *Milwaukee Star*, February 22, 1964, 1.
285. *Milwaukee Sentinel*, March 31, 1964, 11.
286. *Milwaukee Star*, February 22, 1964, 1.
287. *Milwaukee Star*, February 29, 1964, 1; *Milwaukee Star*, March 7, 1964, 1.
288. *Milwaukee Journal*, March 17, 1964, 12.
289. *Milwaukee Star*, March 14, 1964, 2; *Milwaukee Star*, March 28, 1964, 1–2; *Milwaukee Star*, April 4, 1964, 1.
290. *Milwaukee Sentinel*, March 24, 1964, 7; *Milwaukee Sentinel*, March 31, 1964, 4.
291. *Milwaukee Star*, February 1, 1964, 1; *Milwaukee Star*, April 25, 1964, 1; *Milwaukee Star*, May 16, 1964, 1.
292. Letter, Nicholas Wagener, Papers of the NAACP, Press Release, May 8, 1964.
293. Letter, Roy Wilkins, Papers of the NAACP, May 14, 1964.
294. Livingston, "Rights Leaders Voice No Plans," accessed through UW–Milwaukee March on Milwaukee—Civil Rights History Project.
295. Ibid.
296. Telegram to Marshall H. Colston from Roy Wilkins, Papers of the NAACP, March 26, 1964, accessed from the Library of Congress.
297. *Milwaukee Sentinel*, April 9, 1964, 4.
298. Ibid.
299. *Chicago Defender*, April 8, 1964, 15.
300. *Milwaukee Journal*, April 8, 1964, 1.
301. *Milwaukee Sentinel*, April 9, 1964, 4.
302. Ibid.
303. Ibid.

304. Ibid.
305. *Milwaukee Star*, April 11, 1964, 1.
306. Ibid.
307. *Milwaukee Star*, April 11, 1964, 3.
308. Ibid.
309. *Milwaukee Star*, April 11, 1964, 4.
310. *Milwaukee Star*, April 25, 1964, 1.
311. *Milwaukee Star*, May 16, 1964, 1.
312. *Milwaukee Star*, April 11, 1964, 3.
313. *Milwaukee Star*, April 18, 1964, 4.
314. *Milwaukee Courier*, July 3, 1964, 3.

Chapter 4

315. Carter, *Politics of Rage*, 247.
316. Ibid., 246–48.
317. Schumacher, *Contest*, 139.
318. Ibid., 143.
319. Ibid.
320. Carter, *Politics of Rage*, 282–86.
321. Ibid., 305.
322. P. Jones, *Selma of the North*, 71.
323. Geenen, *Civil Rights Activism*, 87.
324. P. Jones, *Selma of the North*, 78.
325. Ibid., 73.
326. Ibid., 78.
327. Ibid., 80.
328. Ibid., 101.
329. Ibid., 114–17.
330. Ibid., 122–23.
331. Ibid., 109.
332. Ibid., 127.
333. Gurda, *Making of Milwaukee*, 370.
334. P. Jones, *Selma of the North*, 134.
335. Ibid., 140.
336. Gurda, *Making of Milwaukee*, 371.

337. P. Jones, *Selma of the North*, 168.
338. Ibid., 1.
339. Ibid., 2–4.
340. Ibid., 176.
341. Ibid., 193–96.
342. Ibid., 203–4.
343. Ibid., 205–8.
344. Ibid., 227.
345. Ibid., 229.
346. Ibid., 233.
347. *New York Times*, June 17, 1967, 15.
348. *New York Times*, June 19, 1967, 20.
349. Carter, *Politics of Rage*, 307.
350. Ibid., 330–32.
351. Ibid., 338.
352. O'Donnell, *Playing with Fire*, 191–94.
353. Greenhaw, *Watch Out for George Wallace*, 36.
354. Schumacher, *Contest*, 202.
355. Carlson, *George C. Wallace*, 128.
356. Ibid., 128–29.
357. O'Donnell, *Playing with Fire*, 194–45.
358. Ibid., 379.
359. Schumacher, *Contest*, 203.
360. *Milwaukee Journal*, April 3, 1968, 1.
361. *Milwaukee Sentinel*, April 3, 1968, 3.
362. *Milwaukee Sentinel*, September 6, 1968, 14.
363. *Milwaukee Sentinel*, September 13, 1968, 12.
364. *Milwaukee Sentinel*, September 13, 1968, 1.
365. *Milwaukee Sentinel*, September 13, 1968, 12.
366. *Janesville Daily Gazette*, September 13, 1968, 1.
367. *Milwaukee Journal*, September 13, 1968, 1
368. *Milwaukee Sentinel*, September 13, 1968, 5.
369. *Capital Times*, September 13, 1968, 1; *Janesville Daily Gazette*, September 13, 1968, 1.
370. *Stevens Point Journal*, September 14, 1968, 2.
371. *Waukesha Daily Freeman*, September 13, 1968, 22.
372. *Milwaukee Sentinel*, September 13, 1968, 14.
373. Ibid.

374. *Milwaukee Sentinel*, September 13, 1968, 5.
375. *Green Bay Press-Gazette*, September 13, 1968, 1; *Racine Journal Times*, September 13, 1968, 1.
376. *New York Times*, September 13, 1968, 51.
377. *Stevens Point Journal*, September 14, 1968, 2.
378. *Milwaukee Sentinel*, September 13, 1968, 1.
379. *Milwaukee Sentinel*, September 13, 1968, 12.
380. *Green Bay Press-Gazette*, September 13, 1968, 1; *Kenosha News*, September 13, 1968, 1.
381. *Capital Times*, September 13, 1968, 1.
382. *Milwaukee Journal*, September 13, 1968, 2.
383. *Waukesha Daily Freeman*, September 13, 1968, 21.
384. *Milwaukee Sentinel*, September 13, 1968, 14.
385. *Waukesha Daily Freeman*, September 13, 1968, 21.
386. *Janesville Press-Gazette*, September 13, 1968, 1.
387. *Green Bay Press Gazette*, September 13, 1968, 1; *Portage Daily Register*, September 13, 1968, 1.
388. *Milwaukee Journal*, September 13, 1968, 2.
389. *Milwaukee Sentinel*, September 13, 1968, 12.
390. *Waukesha Daily Freeman*, September 13, 1968, 21.
391. *Milwaukee Sentinel*, September 13, 1968, 5.
392. Ibid., 14.
393. Ibid., 1, 5.
394. *Eau Claire Daily Telegram*, October 21, 1968, 5.
395. *Waukesha Daily Freeman*, October 21, 1968, 12.
396. *Milwaukee Journal*, October 17, 1968, 3
397. *Oshkosh Sunday Times*, October 20, 1968, 2; *Oshkosh Northwestern*, October 21, 1968, 3.
398. *Oshkosh Northwestern*, October 22, 1968, 1.
399. Ibid., 15; *Milwaukee Sentinel*, October 22, 1968, 1.
400. *Fond du Lac Reporter*, October 22, 1968, 1.
401. Ibid.
402. *Appleton Post Crescent*, October 22, 1968, 6.
403. *Appleton Post Crescent*, October 22, 1968, 1.
404. *Oshkosh Northwestern*, October 22, 1968, 1.
405. *Appleton Post Crescent*, October 22, 1968, 6.
406. *Fond du Lac Reporter*, October 22, 1968, 1; *Appleton Post Crescent*, October 22, 1968, 6.
407. *Appleton Post Crescent*, October 22, 1968, 1.

408. *Appleton Post Crescent*, October 22, 1968, 6; *Stevens Point Journal*, October 22, 1968, 2.
409. *Portage Daily Register*, October 23, 1968, 1.
410. *Waukesha Daily Freeman*, October 24, 1968, 16.
411. *Janesville Gazette*, October 25, 1968, 12.
412. *Appleton Post Crescent*, October 22, 1968, 1; *Fond du Lac Reporter*, October 23, 1968, 2.
413. *Kenosha News*, October 23, 1968, 1.
414. *Milwaukee Journal*, October 23, 1968, 1.
415. *Appleton Post Crescent*, October 22, 1968, 1.
416. *Milwaukee Journal*, October 23, 1968, 1.
417. *Milwaukee Sentinel*, October 23, 1968, 1.
418. *Racine Journal Times*, October 22, 1968, 1, 4.
419. *Milwaukee Journal*, October 23, 1968, 1.
420. *Milwaukee Journal*, October 23, 1968, 3.
421. *Kenosha News*, October 23, 1968, 1.
422. Ibid.; *Racine Journal Times*, October 23, 1968, 1.
423. *Kenosha News*, October 23, 1968, 1.
424. *Stevens Point Journal*, October 23, 1968, 1.
425. *Racine Journal Times*, October 23, 1968, 4.
426. *Milwaukee Sentinel*, October 23, 1968, 13.
427. *Oshkosh Northwestern*, October 23, 1968, 4.
428. Ibid.
429. *Waukesha Daily Freeman*, October 26, 1968, 5.
430. *Sheboygan Press*, November 1, 1968, 7.
431. *Milwaukee Sentinel*, August 12, 1968, 14.
432. *Fond du Lac Reporter*, October 19, 1968, 5.
433. *La Crosse Tribune*, October 21, 1968, 5.
434. *Fond du Lac Reporter*, October 22, 1968, 12.
435. *Milwaukee Sentinel*, October 22, 1968, 10.
436. *Wisconsin Rapids Daily Tribune*, October 22, 1968, 4.
437. *Green Bay Press Gazette*, October 25, 1968, 4.
438. *La Crosse Tribune*, October 25, 1968, 4.
439. *Waukesha Daily Freeman*, November 1, 1968, 4.
440. *Wausau Daily Herald*, November 2, 1968, 4.
441. Ibid.
442. Vel Phillips Papers, Correspondence Box 10, 22.
443. *Racine Journal Times*, October 19, 1968, 8; *Neenah News Record*, October 21, 1968; *Marshfield News Herald*, October 24, 1968, 2.

444. *Milwaukee Journal*, September 16, 1968, 4.

445. *Milwaukee Sentinel*, August 28, 1968, 16.

446. *Racine Journal Times*, September 5, 1968, 1.

447. *Racine Journal Times*, October 20, 1968, 12.

448. *Eau Claire Leader Telegram*, October 22, 1968, 4.

449. Ibid.

450. *Milwaukee Journal*, October 23, 1968, 8.

451. *Green Bay Press Gazette*, October 25, 1968, 4.

452. *Milwaukee Journal*, October 25, 1968, 4.

453. *Racine Journal Times*, October 25, 1968, 2.

454. *Wisconsin Jewish Chronicle*, October 25, 1968, 8.

455. *Capital Times*, October 26, 1968, 24; *Capital Times*, November 2, 1968, 4.

456. *Wisconsin Rapids Daily Tribune*, November 1, 1968, 4.

457. *Appleton Post Crescent*, September 15, 1968, 12.

458. *Oshkosh Northwestern*, October 19, 1968, 21.

459. *Milwaukee Journal*, October 21, 1968, 3.

460. *Neenah News Record*, October 23, 1968, 1.

461. *Milwaukee Courier*, October 5, 1968, 4.

462. Ibid.

463. Ibid.

464. Ibid.

465. Ibid.

466. Ibid.

467. *Milwaukee Courier*, October 5, 1968, 4.

468. *Milwaukee Star*, September 28, 1968, 4

469. *Wisconsin State Journal*, October 23, 1968, 5.

470. *Milwaukee Star*, October 12, 1968, 4.

471. Ibid.

472. Ibid.

473. Lesher, *George Wallace*, 393.

474. Ibid., 427.

475. Schumacher, *Contest*, 314.

476. Ibid., 314–15.

477. Fowler, *Wisconsin Votes*, 189–90.

478. Carter, *Politics of Rage*, 364; *Eau Claire Leader Telegram*, October 22, 1968, 4.

479. Fowler, *Wisconsin Votes*, 190.

480. *Appleton Post-Crescent*, November 6, 1968, 18.

481. Lesher, *George Wallace*, 428.

Chapter 5

482. P. Jones, *Selma of the North*, 242.
483. Ibid., 244–46.
484. Geenen, *Civil Rights Activism*, 70–71.
485. Ibid., 71–72.
486. P. Jones, *Selma of the North*, 249.
487. Ibid.
488. Ibid., 250.
489. Carter, *Politics of Rage*, 417.
490. Ibid., 418.
491. Ibid., 425.
492. Fowler, *Wisconsin Votes*, 192.
493. Carlson, *George C. Wallace*, 144.
494. Ibid., 175.
495. Carter, *Politics of Rage*, 427.
496. Greenhaw, *Watch Out for George Wallace*, 49–50.
497. Frederick, *Stand Up for Alabama*, 338.
498. Lesher, *George Wallace*, 477.
499. *Wisconsin Rapids Tribune*, March 23, 1972, 3.
500. *Milwaukee Journal*, March 23, 1972, 3.
501. *Manitowoc Herald-Times*, March 23, 1972, 21.
502. *Chippewa Herald-Telegram*, March 23, 1972, 9; *Waukesha Daily Freeman*, March 24, 1972, 1.
503. *Milwaukee Journal*, March 24, 1972, 1.
504. *Milwaukee Journal*, March 24, 1972, 26.
505. *Capital Times*, March 24, 1972, 1; *Wisconsin State Journal*, March 26, 1972, 6.
506. *Milwaukee Journal*, March 24, 1972, 26; *Milwaukee Sentinel*, March 24, 1972, 20.
507. *Milwaukee Journal*, March 24, 1972, 26.
508. Ibid.; *Kenosha News*, March 24, 1972, 2.
509. *Milwaukee Journal*, March 24, 1972, 26.
510. Ibid., 1, 26.
511. Ibid.
512. *Kenosha News*, March 24, 1972, 2.
513. *Milwaukee Journal*, March 24, 1972, 1, 26.
514. *Capital Times*, March 28, 1972, 5.
515. *Milwaukee Journal*, March 29, 1972, 2.

516. *Capital Times*, March 28, 1972, 5.

517. *Chippewa Herald Telegram*, March 28, 1972, 2.

518. *Green Bay Press Gazette*, March 28, 1972, 1.

519. Ibid.

520. Ibid.

521. Ibid., 2.

522. *Milwaukee Journal*, March 29, 1972, 2.

523. *Milwaukee Sentinel*, March 29, 1972, 10.

524. *Wisconsin Rapids Daily Tribune*, March 29, 1972, 3.

525. *Milwaukee Journal*, March 29, 1972, 2.

526. *La Crosse Tribune*, March 29, 1972, 1.

527. Ibid.

528. Ibid.

529. Ibid.

530. *Appleton Post Crescent*, March 29, 1972, 1.

531. *Milwaukee Journal*, March 30, 1972, 32.

532. *Appleton Post Crescent*, March 30, 1972, 1.

533. *Milwaukee Journal*, March 30, 1972, 32.

534. *Oshkosh Northwestern*, March 30, 1972, 2.

535. *Appleton Post Crescent*, March 30, 1972, 1.

536. *Milwaukee Journal*, March 31, 1972, 12.

537. Ibid.; *Wisconsin Rapids Tribune*, March 31, 1972, 3.

538. Thompson, *Fear and Loathing*, 119, 124.

539. Ibid., 137

540. Ibid., 139

541. Ibid.

542. *Milwaukee Journal*, March 31, 1972, 12.

543. Carter, *Politics of Rage*, 428.

544. Ibid.

545. *Milwaukee Journal*, March 31, 1972, 12; *Racine Journal Times*, March 31, 1972, 1.

546. *Racine Journal Times*, March 31, 1972, 1.

547. *Eau Claire Leader Telegram*, April 1, 1972, 1; *Chippewa Falls Herald Telegram*, April 3, 1972, 1.

548. *Milwaukee Sentinel*, April 1, 1972, 6.

549. *Chippewa Falls Herald Telegram*, April 2, 1972, 4.

550. *Milwaukee Journal*, April 2, 1972, 5.

551. *Marshfield News Herald*, April 1, 1972, 1.

552. *Milwaukee Journal*, April 2, 1972, 2.

553. *Wausau Daily Herald*, April 3, 1972, 5.
554. *Fond du Lac Reporter*, April 4, 1972, 1.
555. *Milwaukee Journal*, April 4, 1972, 4.
556. *Milwaukee Sentinel*, April 4, 1972, 2.
557. Ibid.
558. *Sheboygan Press*, April 4, 1972, 3.
559. Ibid.
560. Lesher, *George Wallace*, 477; *Milwaukee Journal*, April 5, 1972, 1.
561. Carter, *Politics of Rage*, 428.
562. *Capital Times*, April 5, 1972, 3; *Wisconsin Rapids Daily Tribune*, April 5, 1972, 1.
563. *Appleton Post-Crescent*, April 5, 1972, 1.
564. *Milwaukee Sentinel*, April 6, 1972, 22.
565. *Chippewa Herald Telegram*, April 5, 1972, 2.
566. Ibid.
567. *Milwaukee Journal*, April 5, 1972, 20.
568. Carlson, *George C. Wallace*, 146.
569. *La Crosse Tribune*, April 9, 1972, 13.
570. *Oshkosh Northwestern*, March 24, 1972, 1.
571. Ibid.
572. Ibid.
573. *Milwaukee Journal*, March 30, 1972, 32.
574. *Waukesha Daily Freeman*, March 25, 1972, 6.
575. *Marshfield News Herald*, April 3, 1972, 12.
576. *Sheboygan Press*, April 3, 1972, 17.
577. *Wisconsin State Journal*, March 29, 1972, 3.
578. *Wausau Herald*, March 30, 1972, 4.
579. *Milwaukee Journal*, March 28, 1972, 2.
580. *Milwaukee Journal*, March 29, 1972, 2.
581. *Milwaukee Journal*, March 30, 1972, 4.
582. *Portage Daily Register*, March 23, 1972, 5.
583. *Chippewa Herald Telegram*, March 29, 1972, 4.
584. *Fox Lake Representative*, March 23, 1972, 2.
585. *Kenosha News*, March 24, 1972, 4.
586. *Wisconsin State Journal*, March 26, 1972, 12.
587. *Green Bay Press Gazette*, March 27, 1972, 4.
588. *Milwaukee Sentinel*, March 27, 1972, 11.
589. *Milwaukee Journal*, March 28, 1972, 13; *Racine Journal Times*, March 30, 1972, 10.

590. *Green Bay Press Gazette*, March 30, 1972, 6.

591. *Green Bay Press Gazette*, March 30, 1972, 4.

592. *Capital Times*, April 1, 1972, 22.

593. *Milwaukee Journal*, April 3, 1972, 12.

594. *Milwaukee Sentinel*, March 21, 1972, 1.

595. *Capital Times*, March 24, 1972, 4.

596. Ibid.

597. *Appleton Post Crescent*, March 28, 1972, 3.

598. *Wisconsin State Journal*, April 3, 1972, 12.

599. *Milwaukee Journal*, March 22, 1972, 12.

600. *Capital Times*, March 27, 1972, 33.

601. *Wisconsin Rapids Daily Tribune*, March 27, 1972, 11.

602. *Oshkosh Northwestern*, March 27, 1972, 4.

603. *Green Bay Press Gazette*, March 30, 1972, 2.

604. *Milwaukee Journal*, March 31, 1972, 14.

605. Ibid., 6.

606. *Eau Claire Leader Telegram*, April 1, 1972, 5.

607. *Milwaukee Journal*, April 2, 1972, 22.

608. *Green Bay Press Gazette*, March 30, 1972, 4.

609. *Green Bay Press Gazette*, March 31, 1972, 4.

610. *La Crosse Tribune*, March 31, 1972, 4.

611. *Milwaukee Sentinel*, March 23, 1972, 3.

612. *Capital Times*, March 24, 1972, 4; *Milwaukee Sentinel*, March 24, 1972, 22.

613. *Appleton Post Crescent*, April 1, 1972, 2.

614. *Milwaukee Sentinel*, March 28, 1972, 4.

615. Ibid.

616. *Milwaukee Sentinel*, March 29, 1972, 1.

617. *Wisconsin State Journal*, March 28, 1972, 2.

618. *Wisconsin Rapids Daily Tribune*, March 27, 1972, 11.

619. *Milwaukee Journal*, March 25, 1972, 10.

620. *Milwaukee Journal*, March 28, 1972, 12.

621. *Milwaukee Sentinel*, March 28, 1972, 4.

622. Vel Phillips Papers, Teaching Box 3, 44.

623. *Milwaukee Sentinel*, April 4, 1972, 5.

624. Ibid.; *Stevens Point Journal*, April 4, 1972, 3.

625. *Appleton Post Crescent* March 30, 1972, 5.

626. Ibid., 5.

627. *Milwaukee Courier*, March 25, 1972, 3.

628. *Milwaukee Star*, March 23, 1972, 3.

629. Ibid.

630. *Milwaukee Courier*, March 23, 1972, 6.

631. *Milwaukee Courier*, March 25, 1972, 3.

632. Ibid.

633. Carter, *Politics of Rage*, 419–22, 426–29, 433–37.

634. Ibid., 448–50.

Chapter 6

635. P. Jones, *Selma of the North*, 250.

636. Ibid.

637. Geenen, *Civil Rights Activism*, 90.

638. Frederick, *Stand Up for Alabama*, 349.

639. Carlson, *George C. Wallace*, 204.

640. Carter, *Politics of Rage*, 456.

641. Ibid., 458.

642. Greenhaw, *Watch Out for George Wallace*, 20.

643. Carter, *Politics of Rage*, 457.

644. Carlson, *George C. Wallace*, 206.

645. Greenhaw, *Watch Out for George Wallace*, 80.

646. Carlson, *George C. Wallace*, 248.

647. Ibid., 249.

648. Ibid.

649. Fowler, *Wisconsin Votes*, 192.

650. *Chippewa Herald Telegram*, March 25, 1976, 1.

651. *Milwaukee Journal*, March 29, 1976, 4; *Wisconsin State Journal*, March 30, 1976, 3.

652. *Milwaukee Journal*, March 29, 1976, 4.

653. *Capital Times*, March 27, 1976, 2.

654. *Appleton Post Crescent*, February 27, 1976, 1.

655. Ibid.; *Milwaukee Sentinel*, March 27, 1976, 1.

656. *Wisconsin State Journal*, March 30, 1976, 3.

657. *Milwaukee Journal*, March 27, 1976, 1; *Wisconsin State Journal*, March 27, 1976, 1.

658. *Appleton Post Crescent*, March 27, 1976, 10; *La Crosse Tribune*, March 27, 1976, 2.

659. *Milwaukee Journal*, March 27, 1976, 24; *Kenosha News*, March 27, 1976, 5.

660. *Milwaukee Journal*, March 27, 1976, 1.

661. Ibid.
662. *Kenosha News*, March 27, 1976, 5.
663. *Milwaukee Journal*, March 27, 1976, 1.
664. *Milwaukee Sentinel*, March 27, 1976, 2.
665. *Milwaukee Journal*, March 27, 1976, 2.
666. *Chippewa Herald Telegram*, March 27, 1976, 1.
667. *Capital Times*, March 27, 1976, 1, 2.
668. *Milwaukee Journal*, March 28, 1976, 4.
669. *Milwaukee Sentinel*, March 28, 1976, 2.
670. *Milwaukee Journal*, March 29, 1976, 2.
671. *Milwaukee Journal*, March 27, 1976, 2.
672. *Chippewa Herald Telegram*, March 28, 1976, 2.
673. *Wausau Daily Herald*, March 30, 1976, 1.
674. *La Crosse Tribune*, March 28, 1976, 1.
675. Ibid.
676. *La Crosse Tribune*, March 28, 1976, 1.
677. *Green Bay Press Gazette*, March 30, 1976, 1.
678. *Milwaukee Journal*, March 30, 1976, 4.
679. *Green Bay Press Gazette*, March 30, 1976, 1, 2; *Milwaukee Sentinel*, March 30, 1976, 11.
680. *Milwaukee Journal*, March 30, 1976, 4.
681. Ibid.
682. *Capital Times*, March 30, 1976, 1.
683. Ibid.
684. *Capital Times*, March 31, 1976, 1.
685. Ibid.
686. *Wisconsin State Journal*, March 31, 1976, 6.
687. *Milwaukee Journal*, March 31, 1976, 15; *Milwaukee Sentinel*, March 31, 1976, 1.
688. *Milwaukee Journal*, March 31, 1976, 15.
689. Ibid., 1.
690. *Wisconsin State Journal*, March 31, 1976, 6.
691. *Milwaukee Journal*, March 31, 1976, 1.
692. Ibid., 15.
693. *Capital Times*, April 1, 1976, 4.
694. *New York Times*, April 3, 1976, 12.
695. *Manitowoc Herald Times*, April 1, 1976, 5.
696. *Milwaukee Sentinel*, April 1, 1976, 12; *Wausau Daily Herald*, April 1, 1976, 1.

697. *Eau Claire Leader Telegram*, April 1, 1976, 1; *Milwaukee Journal*, April 1, 1976, 6.

698. *Fond du Lac Reporter*, April 2, 1976, 5.

699. *Milwaukee Journal*, April 2, 1976, 10; *Portage Daily Register*, April 2, 1976, 3.

700. *Milwaukee Sentinel*, April 1, 1976, 12.

701. Ibid.

702. *Milwaukee Sentinel*, April 3, 1976, 10.

703. *Portage Daily Register*, April 5, 1976, 2.

704. *Milwaukee Journal*, April 5, 1976, 2.

705. *Sheboygan Press*, April 6, 1976, 22.

706. *Milwaukee Journal*, April 6, 1976, 1.

707. *Capital Times*, April 7, 1976, 2.

708. *Milwaukee Sentinel*, April 9, 1976, 4.

709. *Capital Times*, April 7, 1976, 3.

710. *Milwaukee Sentinel*, April 7, 1976, 2; *Sheboygan Press*, April 7, 1976, 14.

711. *Milwaukee Journal*, April 7, 1976, 2.

712. *Milwaukee Sentinel*, April 7, 1976, 18.

713. Carlson, *George C. Wallace*, 252.

714. *Oshkosh Northwestern*, March 26, 1976, 2; *Milwaukee Sentinel*, March 26, 1972, 1.

715. *Kenosha News*, March 30, 1976, 3; *Lake Geneva Regional News*, March 25, 1976, 2.

716. *Capital Times*, March 27, 1976, 2.

717. *Fond du Lac Reporter*, April 1, 1976, 3.

718. *Racine Journal Times*, April 4, 1976, 2

719. *Wisconsin Jewish Chronicle*, April 1, 1976, 2.

720. *Milwaukee Journal*, March 31, 1976, 12.

721. *La Crosse Tribune*, April 1, 1976, 3.

722. *Milwaukee Sentinel*, April 1, 1976, 12.

723. *Capital Times*, April 1, 1976, 3.

724. *Wisconsin State Journal*, April 2, 1976, 4.

725. *Milwaukee Sentinel*, April 2, 1976, 6.

726. *Green Bay Press Gazette*, March 29, 1976, 12.

727. *Capital Times*, April 1, 1976, 8.

728. *Capital Times*, April 2, 1976, 6.

729. *Wausau Daily Herald*, April 3, 1976, 15.

730. *La Crosse Tribune*, April 3, 1976, 12.

731. *Racine Journal Times*, April 7, 1976, 14.

732. Ibid.

733. *Milwaukee Journal*, March 26, 1976, 4.
734. *Milwaukee Courier*, March 27, 1976, 5.
735. *Milwaukee Star Times*, April 1, 1976, 4.
736. *Milwaukee Courier*, April 3, 1976, 4..
737. Carter, *Politics of Rage*, 462–63.
738. Ibid., bookflap.
739. P. Jones, *Selma of the North*, 250.
740. W. Jones, *Wallace Story*, 193.
741. Lee, "Jackson Likens Walker to Wallace."

BIBLIOGRAPHY

Articles

Brautigam, Richard. "Wallace Sees Race Feeling in Wisconsin." *Capital Times*, February 19, 1964.

Conway, M. Margaret. "The White Backlash Reexamined: Wallace and the 1964. Primaries." *Social Science Quarterly* 49, no. 3 (1968): 710–19.

Haney, Richard C. "Wallace in Wisconsin: The Presidential Primary of 1964." *Wisconsin Magazine of History* 61, no. 4 (Summer 1978): 258–78.

Leahy, Stephen M. "Polish Reaction to the Civil Rights Movement in Milwaukee, 1963–1965." *Polish American Studies* 63, no. 1 (2006): 35–56.

Lee, MJ. "Jackson Likens Walker to Wallace." *Politico*, June 5, 2012.

Livingston, Charles J. "Rights Leaders Voice No Plans to Counteract Wallace's Anti-Negro, Anti-Rights Campaign of Distortion Exploitation." *Associate Negro Press*, April 13, 1964.

"Milwaukee Catholics Brand Wallace 'Moral Evil.'" *Jet Magazine*, April 1964.

Wisconsin State Historical Society. "Black History in Wisconsin." https://www.wisconsinhistory.org/Records/Article/CS502.

Books

Baker, H. Robert. *The Rescue of Joshua Glover: A Fugitive Slave, the Constitution, and the Coming of the Civil War*. Athens: Ohio University Press, 2006.

Carlson, Jody. *George C. Wallace and the Politics of Powerlessness: The Wallace Campaigns for the Presidency, 1964–1976.* New Brunswick, NJ: Transaction Books, 1981.

Carter, Dan T. *The Politics of Rage: George Wallace, the Origins of the New Conservatism, and the Transformation of American Politics.* New York: Simon and Schuster, 1995.

Fowler, Robert Booth. *Wisconsin Votes: An Electoral History.* Madison: University of Wisconsin Press, 2008.

Frederick, Jeffrey. *Stand Up for Alabama Governor George Wallace.* Tuscaloosa: University of Alabama Press, 2010.

Geenen, Paul H. *Civil Rights Activism in Milwaukee: South Side Struggles in the 60s and 70s.* Charleston, SC: The History Press, 2014.

Greenhaw, Wayne. *Watch Out for George Wallace.* Englewood Cliffs, NJ: Prentice-Hall, 1976.

Gregory, James N. *The Southern Diaspora: How the Great Migrations of Black and White Southerners Transformed America.* Chapel Hill: University of North Carolina Press, 2005.

Gurda, John. *Making of Milwaukee.* Milwaukee, WI: Milwaukee County Historical Society, 2018.

Jones, Patrick D. *The Selma of the North: Civil Rights Insurgency in Milwaukee.* Cambridge, MA: Harvard University Press, 2010.

Jones, William Grover. *The Wallace Story.* Northport, AL: American Southern Publishing Company, 1966.

Lesher, Stephan. *George Wallace: American Populist.* Reading, MA: Addison-Wesley, 1995.

McDonald, Walter T., and Ruby West Jackson. *Finding Freedom: The Untold Story of Joshua Glover, Runaway Slave.* Madison: Wisconsin Historical Society Press, 2007.

O'Donnell, Lawrence. *Playing with Fire.* New York: Penguin USA, 2018.

Schumacher, Michael. *The Contest: The 1968 Election and the War for America's Soul.* Minneapolis: University of Minnesota Press, 2019.

Thompson, Hunter S. *Fear and Loathing on the Campaign Trail '72.* New York: Simon & Schuster, 2014.

Documents

CORE Records, Box 1, Folder 7, Miscellaneous, Mississippi, George Wallace, and Wisconsin State Conference, 1964

Papers of the NAACP, Part 24, Special Subjects, 1956–1965, Series C: Life
    Memberships-Zangrando
Vel Phillips Papers, Teaching Box 3, p. 44, Correspondence Box 10, p. 22.

Newspapers
(1964–1976)

Appleton Post-Crescent
Associated Negro Press
Capital Times
Chicago Defender
Chippewa Herald-Telegram
Eau Claire Daily Telegram
Fond du Lac Reporter
Fox Lake Representative
Green Bay Press-Gazette
Janesville Daily Gazette
Kenosha News
La-Crosse Tribune
Lake Geneva Regional News
Manitowoc Herald-Times
Marshfield News-Herald
Milwaukee Courier
Milwaukee Journal

Milwaukee Sentinel
Milwaukee Star
Neenah News-Record
New York Times
Oshkosh Northwestern
Oshkosh Sunday Times
Portage Daily Register
Racine Journal-Times
Sheboygan Press
Stevens Point Journal
UWM Post
Waukesha Daily Freeman
Wausau Daily Herald
Wisconsin Jewish Chronicle
Wisconsin Rapids Daily Tribune
Wisconsin State Journal

ABOUT THE AUTHOR

Historian Ben Hubing, a high school educator and educational consultant, is the recipient of a number of awards, including the James Madison Foundation Fellowship and the Herb Kohl Teaching Fellowship. He earned his bachelor's degree from the University of Wisconsin–Madison and a master's in teaching from Cardinal Stritch University. He earned a master's degree in history at University of Wisconsin–Milwaukee, with a focus on intersections of civil rights, politics and constitutional history. Hubing lives in Shorewood, Wisconsin, with his wife, Nickie, and their three children.

Visit us at
www.historypress.com